Testing KS3 ENGLISH

Skills & Practice

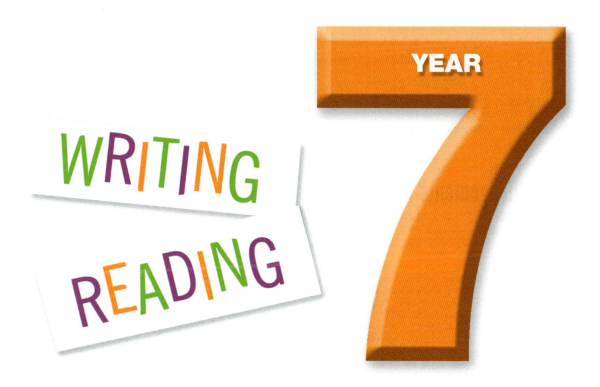

WRITING
READING

YEAR 7

Ray Barker ◆ Christine Moorcroft

Text © Ray Barker and Christine Moorcroft 2003
Original illustrations © Nelson Thornes Ltd 2003

The right of Ray Barker and Christine Moorcroft to be identified as authors of this work
has been asserted by them in accordance with the Copyright, Designs and Patents Act 1988.

All rights reserved. No part of this publication may be reproduced or transmitted in any form or by any
means, electronic or mechanical, including photocopy, recording or any information storage and retrieval
system, without permission in writing from the publisher or under licence from the Copyright Licensing
Agency Limited, of 90 Tottenham Court Road, London W1T 4LP.

Any person who commits any unauthorised act in relation to this publication may be liable to criminal
prosecution and civil claims for damages.

First published in 2003 by:

Nelson Thornes Ltd
Delta Place
27 Bath Road
CHELTENHAM
GL53 7TH
United Kingdom

03 04 05 06 07 / 10 9 8 7 6 5 4 3 2 1

A catalogue record for this book is available from the British Library

ISBN 0 7487 7133 6

Typeset by Barking Dog Art
Developed and produced by Start to Finish
Printed and bound in Italy by Canale

Acknowledgements

The tests, questions and advice in this series are based upon official test materials sent to schools, but are not reproductions of these tests.
The official testing process is supported by guidance and training for teachers by the Qualifications and Curriculum Authority (QCA) to
use in setting and marking tests and interpreting results. The results achieved by taking the tests in this book may not be the same as are
achieved in the official tests.

We gratefully acknowledge permission to include the following copyright material: **Test Paper 1:** Edward Blishen: *Roaring Boys:
A Schoolmaster's Agony* (Thames & Hudson, 1955), copyright © the Estate of Edward Blishen, reprinted by permission of A. M. Heath & Co.
Ltd. on behalf of the Estate; Roger McGough: 'First Day at School' from *In the Glassroom* (Jonathan Cape, 1976), copyright © Roger
McGough 1976, reprinted by permission of PFD on behalf of the author; extract from 'The National Debate on Education' published
on Education in Scotland www.scotland.gov.uk website is Crown copyright material and is reproduced under Class Licence Number
CO2W0002214 with the permission of the Controller of HMSO and the Queen's Printer for Scotland; **Test Paper 2:** Rosemary Sutcliffe:
extract from *Beowulf: Dragon Slayer* (Bodley Head, 1961), reprinted by permission of The Random House Group Ltd; Richard Carrington:
extract from *Mermaids and Mastodons: A book of Natural and Unnatural History* (Chatto & Windus, 1957), reprinted by permission of
The Random House Group Ltd; **Test Paper 3:** William Mayne: extract from *Plot Night* (Hamish Hamilton, 1963/1977), reprinted by
permission of David Higham Associates; Les Ray: 'Diwali in Kerala', first published here by permission of the author; **Test Paper 4:**
Rudyard Kipling: 'The Way Through the Woods' from *The Definitive Edition of Rudyard Kipling's Verse*, reprinted by permission of A. P. Watt
Ltd. on behalf of The National Trust for Places of Historical Interest or Natural Beauty; extract from 'Britain's rainforests need protecting
now' published on www.woodland-trust.org.uk website, reprinted by permission of The Woodland Trust; **Test Paper 5:** Pam Gidney: 'A
Perfect Match' first published in David Orme (ed): *You'll Never Walk Alone* (Macmillan, 1995), reprinted by permission of the author; Paul
Fraser: 'Magpies come from behind to beat Charlton', *The Northern Echo*, 26.10.02, reprinted by permission of North of England
Newspapers, Newsquest (North East) Ltd; **Test Paper 6:** Kevin Crossley-Holland: extract from *The Seeing-Stone* (Orion Children's Books,
2000), reprinted by permission of The Orion Publishing Group; Tom Leonard: 'Unrelated Incidents 3' from *Intimate Voices: Selected Works*
(Galloping Dog Press, 1984), reprinted by permission of the author; Martin Wainright: 'Chicken fat to power lorries', *The Guardian*,
29.10.02, copyright © The Guardian 2002, reprinted by permission of Guardian Newspapers Ltd.

Although we have tried to obtain copyright permissions before publication this has not been possible in every case. If notified, the publisher
agrees to make the necessary arrangements to rectify the situation.

Illustrations by: Linda Jeffrey, pages 67, 71, 75, 83, 87, 91; **Carol Jonas**, pages 5, 9, 15, 22, 26, 31;
Ruth Palmer, pages 38, 43, 48, 55, 58, 61.

Contents

Test Paper 1: School

Reading test 1: Some basics ... from *Roaring Boys* by Edward Blishen 4

Reading test 2: Extending your skills ... 'First Day at School' by Roger McGough 9

Reading test 3: Over to you ... from 'Education in Scotland', Scottish Executive website . . 14

Writing test: The real thing 19

Test Paper 2: Monsters

Reading test 1: Some basics ... from *Dragon Slayer* by Rosemary Sutcliffe 21

Reading test 2: Extending your skills ... 'Loch Ness Monster' from *Mermaids and Mastodons*
by Richard Carrington 26

Reading test 3: Over to you ... from 'The Kraken' by Alfred Lord Tennyson 31

Writing test: The real thing 35

Test Paper 3: Times of celebration

Reading test 1: Some basics ... 'Christmas' from *Life and Literacy* by P J McGeeney 37

Reading test 2: Extending your skills ... from *Plot Night* by William Mayne 43

Reading test 3: Over to you ... 'Diwali in Kerala' by Les Ray 48

Writing test: The real thing 52

Test Paper 4: Woodlands

Reading test 1: Some basics ... from *The Wind in the Willows* by Kenneth Grahame 54

Reading test 2: Extending your skills ... 'The Way Through the Woods' by Rudyard Kipling 58

Reading test 3: Over to you ... from 'Britain's rainforests need protecting now',
Woodland Trust website 61

Writing test: The real thing 65

Test Paper 5: Football

Some basics ... from *A Legend in his Own Time* 67

Extending your skills ... 'A Perfect Match' by Pam Gidney 71

Over to you ... 'Magpies come from behind to beat Charlton'
by Paul Fraser 74

The real thing 80

Test Paper 6: News

Some basics ... from *The Seeing Stone* by Kevin Crossley-Holland 82

Extending your skills ... 'Unrelated Incidents 3' by Tom Leonard 87

Over to you ... 'Chicken fat to power lorries' by Martin Wainwright . . . 91

The real thing 95

Test Paper 1: Reading

School

Some BASICS...

This section of the paper is a test of reading and interpretation, although *how* you communicate information is important. The theme linking these three reading texts is 'School'.

- You have 1 hour and 15 minutes to answer the questions on the three passages.
- You are given 15 minutes' reading time before this.

Reading test 1

Reading and interpreting a passage from *Roaring Boys* by Edward Blishen

This text is taken from a book which tells of the experiences of a new teacher in a London school in the 1940s.

The room was easily traced by the noise that was coming from it. It didn't sound a studious noise. I crept through the door. Enormous boys were everywhere, doing indefensible things. I can't recall much in particular what they were doing; indeed, that was the worst of it – that these improprieties couldn't be nailed down.

I managed to make out that mixed up with these giants was a certain amount of furniture. This consisted, I found, of individual desks; doll's house things that rested on mountainous knees and swayed from side to side. Too negligently or maliciously treated, one would, from time to time, crash to the floor. There were certainly fights going on; and I believe one desk was chasing another. The air was full of pieces of chalk, a strange rain of it.

Feeling invisible, I walked towards the teacher's desk. Not an eye was turned in my direction. I just stood there and looked at them and an awful pointless indignation mounted in me. Was I not a teacher? Had I not been approved by the Ministry itself? Was I really so puny, so ineffective?

"Now, shut up," I shouted. There was a fatal note of pleading in my voice. They took no notice, so I shouted again.

And then I said, "If you don't shut up, I'll …" Now they heard me and an awful silence came, not an obedient silence but a sceptical one. My voice trailed away. If they didn't shut up, I would – what? I was toying inwardly with ideas of thunderbolts, earthquakes, mass executions. But in cold blood I could think of no practical substitute for these dramatic punishments.

A boy leaned back in his desk, indolently far back, and said, "Are you going to try to teach us?" He looked round and laughed. There was a murmur from the back of the room and another laugh.

Some BASICS...

I was shocked to the core. Shocked, stung and frightened. "Yes, I am," I shouted. "And you – you had better shut up."

They all laughed. Then they turned to one another and discussed the matter. A fight began at the back. But what hurt me most was that in the middle of the room sat a very studious-looking boy reading a book. He looked up, raised a wry eyebrow, looked at me, raised his eyebrow higher, and shrugged himself back into his book.

I shouted for a while, but it was beyond me. I hadn't the manner. I was a plain impostor. My blushing and bawling were a joy to them. There was, for a time, pandemonium, like a big scene in an opera being played backwards on a gramophone.

Then, since there had to be some resemblance between this and what I understood to be a lesson, I fumbled for a theme. I had dimly planned, coming down, to ask them where they had got to in history. I could guess now at the answer I might get. Feeling like a cornered film brigand who tries to keep a crowd at bay with a single pistol, I edged towards a cupboard, keeping my face turned towards the class. Out of the corner of an eye I saw the cupboard was, except for crumpled paper, bare. What was I to do?

It struck me that I had in my brief-case a book on Chaucer. It contained a large number of documents of the period. Accounts of street brawls. It seemed apposite. I felt in the case and brought out the book.

It was, alas, very big and looked very academic. "Cor, the Bible," said a voice. "Read any good books lately?" said another. "You hit me with that and I'll tell my dad." "He can read!" And, in falsetto, "Tell us a fairy story!"

"Shut up," I shouted, and desperately turned the leaves. The street brawls eluded me. But here was a bit about fourteenth-century trading regulations. "A long time ago," I roared.

Test Paper 1: Reading

By accident there was silence at this moment. So the voice that shouted "Tell me the old, old story," was very clear indeed. And the shouter was easy to identify. My nerves gave a twitch and I shouted back. "What's your name, you … I'll … Come on, what's your name?"

I had much to learn about this sort of inquisition. "Chumley," he shouted, "Lord Chumley." "Of Chumley Manor," came another voice. My own accent came at me, insolently and indeed, most skilfully exaggerated.

"You'll have to come with me to the headmaster," I howled. To my mind, or rather to the hot whirling chaos that had been my mind, that was a terrible threat. I expected instant capitulation. Instead, the boy chose to consider himself insulted. "You can't prove nothing," he shouted. "I ain't done nothing. You ain't going to get me into trouble."

Questions 1–7 are about *Roaring Boys*

1 Select and copy the words which show how the teacher knew how to find the room.

(1 mark)

Focus: Describe, select and retrieve information and events or ideas from the text. Use quotation and reference to the text.

Notice the words 'select and copy'. You need to find the words and then copy them, using quotation marks.

2 Find and copy three things the teacher noticed as he came into the class.

(2 marks)

Focus: Describe, select and retrieve information and events or ideas from the text. Use quotation and reference to the text.

Notice the words 'find and copy'. This suggests that the examiner is looking for quotations, and not your own words. If you are given a number of things to find, in this case three, do not think that these are all the points. There may be more for you to choose from. Give only three.

Hint: Look up the meaning of the word 'trace' in a dictionary.

6

Some BASICS...

3. 'If you don't shut up, I'll …'. What is the author's purpose in putting the three dots?
   - What effect did this statement have on the boys?
   - Why did it have this effect?
   - Why did this cause a problem for the teacher? **(3 marks)**

   Focus: Deduce, infer and interpret information and events or ideas from the text.

First find the relevant part of the text and read it again. Imagine yourself in the position of this new teacher. Then decide: what might the teacher have been going to say and why didn't he say it?
What were the boys expecting him to say?
What would the teacher have had to do, once he had said something to the boys? Could he have done this?

4. Quote two examples of the writer's use of description which give us a sense of the boys' rebelliousness. **(2 marks)**

   Focus: Describe, select and retrieve information and events or ideas from the text. Use quotation and reference to the text.

Notice that the question asks you to quote. Here you are looking for 'the writer's use of description', so you need to look at the words carefully.
Find places in the passage where he describes what the boys are like and what they do.

5. Explain why the 'studious-looking boy' 'hurt' the author. Look at what he does and what he represents. **(2 marks)**

   Focus: Deduce, infer and interpret information and events or ideas from the text.

Find the relevant part in the passage. Make notes on a chart.

How the boy was different from the rest	
What he was doing	
What he did when the teacher looked at him	
What you think was going through his mind at this point	
How this made the teacher feel	

Test Paper 1: Reading

6 The author asks a series of questions. 'Was I not a teacher? Had I not been approved by the Ministry itself? Was I really so puny, so ineffective?' They are rhetorical questions. What is the effect of these? **(2 marks)**

Focus: Comment on the writer's use of language, grammatical and literary features at word and sentence level.

Find out about rhetorical questions. Why are they different from other questions?
What happens if you answer these questions?

7 The author wants us to be sympathetic towards him and not towards the pupils. Does he succeed?
You should write about:
- whether you find this amusing or not
- the use of language
- what the boys say and do
- what the reader's expectations would be of the situation. **(4 marks)**

Focus: Identify and comment on the writer's purposes and viewpoints, and the effect of the text on the reader.

Think about these points:
What do you think a teacher should be like?
Does the narrator live up to this?
How does this affect the way you feel about him?
Because some of the passage is funny, does this affect the way we feel about the teacher?
Consider the way he writes. Do you find it difficult or easy to read?
Is it a suitable language to use with the pupils described?
Do you sympathise more with the boys? Why?

Test Paper 1: Reading

Extending Your SKILLS...

Reading test 2
Reading and interpreting a poem by Roger McGough

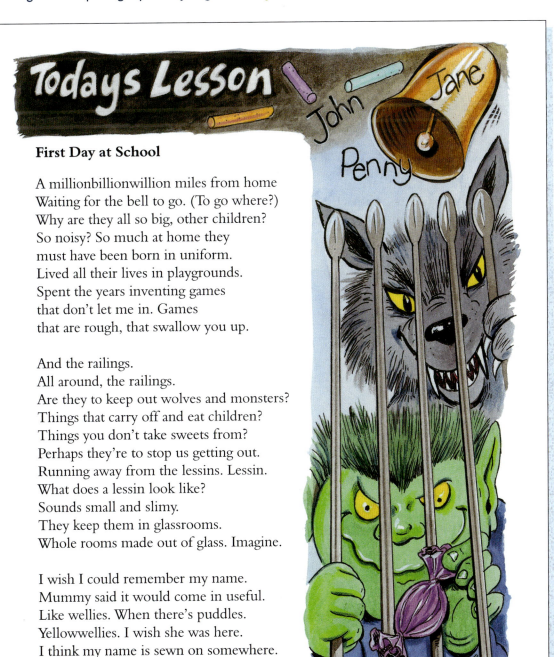

First Day at School

A millionbillionwillion miles from home
Waiting for the bell to go. (To go where?)
Why are they all so big, other children?
So noisy? So much at home they
must have been born in uniform.
Lived all their lives in playgrounds.
Spent the years inventing games
that don't let me in. Games
that are rough, that swallow you up.

And the railings.
All around, the railings.
Are they to keep out wolves and monsters?
Things that carry off and eat children?
Things you don't take sweets from?
Perhaps they're to stop us getting out.
Running away from the lessins. Lessin.
What does a lessin look like?
Sounds small and slimy.
They keep them in glassrooms.
Whole rooms made out of glass. Imagine.

I wish I could remember my name.
Mummy said it would come in useful.
Like wellies. When there's puddles.
Yellowwellies. I wish she was here.
I think my name is sewn on somewhere.
Perhaps the teacher will read it for me.
Tea-cher. The one who makes the tea.

Test Paper 1: Reading

Questions 8–15 are about *First Day at School*

8 Copy and complete the chart to show what the poem tells us.   **(2 marks)**

Setting	
Narrator	
Other characters	
Situation	

Focus: Comment on the structure and organisation of texts, grammatical and presentational features at text level.

Read the poem carefully and make notes in a chart. Summarise this information to answer the question. Look at the setting of the poem, who is there and what the central situation is behind the writing of the poem.

9 Say what you think are the subjects of each of the three verses. Select and copy words to support what you say.   **(2 marks)**

Verse	Subjects	Quotation
1		
2		
3		

Focus: Comment on the structure and organisation of texts, grammatical and presentational features at text level.

The poem is split into three verses. Just like paragraphs, each verse of the poem will be about something different. Make notes about what each verse tells you and then summarise the information until you can see what the **main subjects** of each verse are. Don't bother telling the examiner everything which happens in every verse.

Hint: Don't forget to look at the title for a clue.

Extending Your SKILLS...

10 What do you find strange about the language used in the first line of the poem? **(1 mark)**

   Focus: Deduce, infer and interpret information and events or ideas from the text.

It will be obvious to you that there is a very strange word in the verse. Explain to the examiner why this is strange. However, the poet has obviously written this word for a purpose. Ask yourself: Who is the narrator?
How would this person think and speak? Why?
Do the words give a better impression of the narrator?

11 Copy the chart and place a cross in the four boxes which tell us what the child noticed. **(2 marks)**

Noisy children		Children playing games	
Children wearing wellingtons		Children who are much larger than himself	
Children not wearing uniform		Quiet children	
Puddles in the playground		The school fence	

   Focus: Describe, select and retrieve information and events or ideas from the text. Use quotation and reference to the text.

This question tests how carefully you read. Watch out – this can be tricky! Read the poem and tick if the words tell you these things – and only these things!

12 Explain the following metaphor and its effect: 'Games / that are rough, that swallow you up'. **(2 marks)**

   Focus: Comment on the writer's use of language, grammatical and literary features at word and sentence level.

You have to decide what two things are being compared.
What kind of thing swallows you up?
Does the child like these games or is he scared of them?

Test Paper 1: Reading

Explain what kind of picture the words make in your mind.
There is no 'right' answer. If you can explain why these words create this picture for you, it is as good an answer as anybody else's. But you have to explain why.

Hint: Remember: metaphors are comparisons, but they do not use words such as 'like' or 'as'. They say something **is** something else. Metaphors make pictures in our minds.

---

13 Humour in the poem is created by the confusion of the child over the meaning of words. Select and copy two examples of this. Explain the confusion. **(3 marks)**

Focus: Describe, select and retrieve information and events or ideas from the text. Use quotation and reference to the text.

First quote the words which the child confuses and say what the words should be.
Explain why each one is strange and funny. Is it because of what you know of that thing already?
Is it because it makes you see that thing in a new light?

---

14 Select and copy two examples of statements in the poem which are not complete sentences. Why does the poet do this? What effect does the poet want these to create? Write the statements as complete sentences. Comment on the difference of effect. **(3 marks)**

Focus: Comment on the writer's use of language, grammatical and literary features at word and sentence level.

Poems are structured in a different way from narrative text. However, in this poem there are many statements which are not real sentences. The writer uses full stops but many statements do not contain a subject, an object or a verb.
Notice that you are asked to 'select and copy'. This means you must use quotation marks.
Think about why the poet has written in this style. You need to think about the narrator of the poem. Would he speak in complete sentences all the time? Why not?

Extending Your SKILLS...

15 Explain how the writer communicates the point of view of a child in this poem. You should write about:

- the language used
- the attitudes expressed
- the thoughts developed
- what the child sees and hears
- how the child interprets the world.

(5 marks)

Focus: Identify and comment on the writer's purposes and viewpoints, and the effect of the text on the reader.

The speaker is a child, and part of the fun of this poem is the way he looks at the world of school. Make notes about each of these points. Use a chart.

Language used	
Attitudes	
Thoughts	
Sees and hears	
How the child interprets the world	

This question is worth quite a few marks so you need to express yourself clearly. Write a paragraph about each point. Back up your ideas with quotations from the poem. Much of the information for this question can be found in the other answers in this unit, so don't ignore what you have written before. But don't just copy this out – put it into your own words.

Test Paper 1: Reading

Reading test 3
Reading and interpreting a passage from *Education in Scotland*

The National Debate on Education: the best for ALL our children

WHY?
Education is important for a number of reasons – to support and encourage children and young people in order to help them to live a happy and healthy life; to help them to develop and achieve their ambitions; to prepare them for a creative and productive working life, and to prepare them to be citizens of a changing world. These are only a few of the reasons why we educate young people. It is important to look to the future to develop an education system which meets all of these needs, for all of our children.

WHAT?
To prepare for the future, we need to think about what children should learn. The balance between learning about individual areas of knowledge, and learning the skills with which to apply that knowledge, is important. There will be key things in the future which are important for everyone to learn, such as learning to read. Children can experience many different activities at school in order to help them to become happy, healthy and responsible citizens. What a young person experiences during a school day in the future might be different from today. There are also likely to be specialist areas of interest only to particular individuals.

To be sure that we are helping young people throughout their time at school, it is important to measure how they are progressing. It is also important for young people to be able to display what they have achieved. Different people are talented in different ways, whether that be in traditional academic areas, in practical vocational skills, or in other personal achievements. With this in mind, what sort of information should young people be able to show potential employers?

Learning can be effective and enjoyable when it takes place through physical and other activities. Sport, the arts and music can contribute to many aspects of learning, and can play a major role in helping young people to develop personal attitudes.

WHEN?
Children and young people spend at least 10 years at school. This is longer than many people spend working in one job, or living in one place. The changes which take place in a young person over that decade are probably the most significant of their lifetime. Different people are ready for different experiences at different times – and so there may be ways to organise learning, as well as by

Over to YOU...

age, which help every young person with his or her learning. The age at which children start school is important, as well as the age at which they leave.

The transfers from pre-school to primary school, from primary to secondary school and from school to the rest of their life can be daunting for young people. A change of school, a change of people (both fellow pupils and teachers) and new pressures can all add up to a very challenging experience. There may be different ways in which we can help children and young people to take on these challenges confidently. There may be different ways in which to ensure a minimum amount of disruption to young people, especially in their early teenage years.

The school day begins and ends for many with a bell, and varies from day to day for teachers and for young people. This way of organising the school day may provide the best conditions for learning – but there may be other approaches. Some activities might be particularly suited for the morning, and different ones for the afternoon. The (roughly) 9 to 4, Monday to Friday structure, with a long holiday in the summer, could be the model we see in the future. Equally, there may be other ways to organise the learning and teaching year, week and day which are effective.

WHERE?
Most children and young people go to school – a building with classrooms and corridors. Providing a safe, purpose-built and stimulating environment is important in helping children to learn – that learning environment might look very different in the future.

Some schools are open after the school day has finished – with facilities being used at weekends, evenings and holidays. We could extend the use of school facilities for the wider community – for learning, for socialising or for other activities. Other things might take place in a school which specifically

Test Paper 1: Reading

help with a young person's development. In the long-term future, the way in which schools are organised and managed might look different from today, and we could explore the balance of responsibility between the school and the education authority.

There are places to learn other than schools – in libraries, colleges and universities, at work, in the community, or at home. These locations could help with teaching some subjects and skills more effectively – and there will be different people, as well as teachers, who can help deliver education.

Interaction with other people is an important experience, and school can help children to develop social skills. To make the best of this experience, a good ethos is important in a school: young people have the right to be respected, to feel safe, and to be treated as individuals. The school can be an oasis. It should aim to support children who feel isolated at school, or who have difficult personal circumstances.

Questions 16–21 are about *Education in Scotland*

16 Find and copy four reasons from the first paragraph to say why education is important.

(2 marks)

Focus: Describe, select and retrieve information and events or ideas from the text. Use quotation and reference to the text.

Read the first paragraph again and find the reasons. Notice that you are asked to 'copy', so the examiner is expecting you to quote. You have been asked for 'four reasons'. There may be more: you need to make the choice.

17 In the 'When?' section there are three paragraphs. Each paragraph covers a different topic. Copy the chart and draw a line to match each paragraph to its topic.

(2 marks)

Paragraph 1	Transfer from one school to another
Paragraph 2	The school timetable
Paragraph 3	Years spent at school

Focus: Describe, select and retrieve information and events or ideas from the text. Use quotation and reference to the text.

Over to YOU...

Find the section and read each paragraph. Look for the topic sentences – those which tell you the subject. Draw the lines in pencil first of all in case you change your mind!

18 Explain what the author means by: 'Different people are talented in different ways, whether that be in traditional academic areas, in practical vocational skills, or in other personal achievements.' **(2 marks)**

Focus: Comment on the writer's use of language, grammatical and literary features at word and sentence level.

This question is testing your vocabulary knowledge. In class, although not in an exam, you need to look up words in your dictionary. Concentrate on words such as 'academic' (what parts of school are 'academic'?) and 'vocational' (what do you learn in school which is 'vocational'?)
Make notes and put your ideas together. What is the writer really trying to say?
Write your explanation in short sentences, taking one point at a time.

19 The writer uses a metaphor: 'The school can be an oasis'. Explain the comparison and comment on how well you think it works in the description.

(2 marks)

Focus: Comment on the writer's use of language, grammatical and literary features at word and sentence level.

Decide what is being compared and to what. The metaphor makes a positive statement – a school is a rich educational environment. Think about the characteristics of both parts of the metaphor.

Oasis	School

In what ways are an oasis and a school similar?

Test Paper 1: Reading

20 Suggest what the author might mean by the following statement. Give some examples of the 'other things'. **(2 marks)**

> Other things might take place in a school which specifically help with a young person's development. In the long-term future, the way in which schools are organised and managed might look different from today ...

Focus: Deduce, infer and interpret information and events or ideas from the text.

This question asks you to deduce what the author may really mean, that is, what idea lies behind his or her words.

What other things in school would help a young person to achieve the aims of education as mentioned in the first paragraph? Give some of your ideas. Your ideas will be treated positively if you can express them and they are sensible.

21 Explain the difference in use between the following uses of dashes and hyphens. **(4 marks)**

There are places to learn other than schools – in libraries, colleges and universities, at work, in the community, or at home. These locations could help with teaching some subjects and skills more effectively – and there will be different people, as well as teachers, who can help deliver education.	The transfers from pre-school to primary school ... Providing a safe, purpose-built and stimulating environment is important ...

Focus: Comment on the writer's use of language, grammatical and literary features at word and sentence level.

First decide which are dashes and which are hyphens. Which ones separate ideas? Writers often need to explain things further. Dashes give them the space to do this. Hyphens create new words from two separate words by joining them together.

Hint: Remember: dashes **separate** ideas. They help writers to explain something in more detail. Hyphens **join** words or ideas, often creating new words.

Test Paper 1: Writing

Writing test

These two writing assignments are linked to the theme of 'School'.

Major task

- You should spend about 40 minutes on this.
- There are 30 marks available.

Write a description of what you imagine to be 'the school of the future'.

Think about these points:
- What will the school building be like?
- Will there still be teachers?
- What subjects will you be taught?
- Will everything be taught by computers?
- Will there be robots?
- Why will there be a need to change?

Planning

- Before you start writing, use the format on this page to help you to plan and write notes.
- Allow time to read your work and check your use of language before you finish.

Introduction Will the school be so different? Why is there a need to change?	**The school building** How will this have to adapt to changing circumstances?
Who will teach me? Will I have a teacher? Will there be robots?	**What will I be taught?**
How do I feel about all this? What is good about school now?	**Conclusion**

19

Test Paper 1: Writing

Minor task

- You should spend about 25 minutes on this.
- There are 20 marks available.

Some people believe that the school day should be lengthened and that holidays should be made shorter. Say what you think about these two issues in a letter to a newspaper.

You should write only three paragraphs in order to:
- inform the readers of your views
- persuade them to agree with you.

Do not use the same information as you included in your answer to the major writing task.

Planning

- Before you start writing, use the format on this page to help you to plan and write notes.
- Organise your ideas into three paragraphs only.
- Allow time to read your work and check your use of language before you finish.

Your address on the right-hand side	How will you open the letter? What tone do you want to achieve? Formal? Informal?
Body of the letter I believe that … Back up your case with arguments	**Conclusion** Summarise the important points in the last paragraph
Words to use to persuade people I believe that … It is clear that … Some people say that … However, …	**Ending the letter** If you started 'Dear Sir' or 'Dear Madam' you need to end 'Yours faithfully' If you started 'Dear Mr/Mrs/ Miss/Ms …' you need to end 'Yours sincerely'

Test Paper 2: Reading

Monsters

Some BASICS...

This section of the paper is a test of reading and interpretation, although *how* you communicate information is important. The theme linking these three reading texts is 'Monsters'.

- You have 1 hour and 15 minutes to answer the questions on the three passages.
- You are given 15 minutes' reading time before this.

Reading test 1
Reading and interpreting a passage from *Dragon Slayer* by Rosemary Sutcliffe

This is a version of a story from the Anglo-Saxon poem 'Beowulf'.

In the darkest hour of the spring night Grendel came to Heorot as he had come so many times before, up from his lair and over the high moors, through the mists that seemed to travel with him under the pale moon: Grendel, the Night-Stalker, the Death-Shadow. He came to the foreporch and snuffed about it, and smelled the man-smell, and found that the door which had stood unlatched for him so long was barred and bolted. Snarling in rage that any man should dare attempt to keep him out, he set the flat of his talon-tipped hands against the timbers and burst them in.

Dark as it was, the hall seemed to fill with a monstrous shadow at his coming; a shadow in which Beowulf, half springing up, then holding himself in frozen stillness, could make out no shape nor clear outline save two eyes filled with a wavering greenish flame.

The ghastly corpse-light of his own eyes showed Grendel the shapes of men as it seemed sleeping, and he did not notice among them one who leaned up on his elbow. Laughing in his throat, he reached out and grabbed young Hondscio who lay nearest to him, and almost before his victim had time to cry out, tore him limb from limb and drank the warm blood. Then, while the young warrior's dying shriek still hung upon the air, he reached for another. But this time his hand was met and seized in a grasp such as he had never felt before; a grasp that had in it the strength of thirty men. And for the first time he who had brought fear to so many caught the taste of it himself, knowing that at last he had met his match and maybe his master.

Beowulf leapt from the sleeping bench and grappled him in the darkness; and terror broke over Grendel in full force, the terror of a wild animal trapped; so that he thought no more of his hunting but only of breaking the terrible

Test Paper 2: Reading

hold upon his arm and flying back into the night and the wilderness, and he howled and bellowed as he struggled for his freedom. Beowulf set his teeth and summoned all his strength and tightened his grip until the sinews cracked; and locked together they reeled and staggered up and down the great hall. Trestles and sleeping benches went over with crash on crash as they strained this way and that, trampling even through the last red embers of the dying fire; and the very walls seemed to groan and shudder as though the stout timbers would burst apart. And all the while Grendel snarled and shrieked and Beowulf fought in silence save for his gasping breaths.

Outside, the Danes listened in horror to the turmoil that seemed as though it must split Heorot asunder; and within, the Geats had sprung from their sleeping benches sword in hand, forgetful of their powerlessness against the Troll-kind, but in the dark, lit only by stray gleams of bale-fire from the monster's eyes, they dared not strike for fear of slaying their leader, and when one or other of them did contrive to get in a blow, the sword blade glanced off Grendel's charmed hide as though he were sheathed in dragon scales.

At last, when the hall was wrecked to the walls, the Night-Stalker gathered himself for one last despairing effort to break free. Beowulf's hold was as fierce as ever; yet none the less the two figures burst apart – and Grendel with a frightful shriek staggered to the doorway and through it, and fled wailing into the night, leaving his arm and shoulder torn from the roots in the hero's still unbroken grasp.

Some BASICS...

Questions 1–7 are about *Dragon Slayer*

1   Copy and complete the chart to show what basic information the story gives you.

(1 mark)

Setting	
Time of day	
Season	

Focus: Describe, select and retrieve information and events or ideas from the text. Use quotation and reference to the text.

Read the first paragraph. Note down the relevant information. In the exam, you can underline important words or highlight them in colour.

Hint: If you are not sure of the meanings of some of the words, try to work them out from the context.
You can use a dictionary now but not in an exam!

2   Explain why Grendel the monster was angry at the door of Heorot. What does this show about his view of himself? **(2 marks)**

Focus: Deduce, infer and interpret information and events or ideas from the text.

What had the creature been used to before? Find evidence for this.
What did this show about humans' fear of Grendel?
Who do you think locked the door on Grendel?
What did it signify to the monster?

3   Select and copy the two things which were uppermost in Grendel's mind when he was grasped by Beowulf. **(2 marks)**

Focus: Describe, select and retrieve information and events or ideas from the text. Use quotation and reference to the text.

Notice that the question asks you to 'select and copy', so you will need to take the actual words from the passage and use quotation marks.

23

Test Paper 2: Reading

4   The following are the subjects of the six paragraphs. Copy the boxes and write the appropriate letter in the correct box to show the structure of the passage.

(3 marks)

     A. The monster flees, leaving a limb behind.
     B. Beowulf fights Grendel.
     C. Grendel approaches and breaks down the door of the Hall.
     D. Beowulf's friends try to help.
     E. Grendel kills Hondscio but Beowulf attacks.
     F. The monster enters the Hall.

1	2	3	4	5	6

Focus: Comment on the structure and organisation of texts, grammatical and presentational features at text level.

Look carefully at the key ideas of each paragraph. Remember, each paragraph should have a topic sentence. Don't bother with all the details – what is the author really trying to make us understand in the paragraphs?

5   The writer uses very accurate and effective verbs, for example:

> Beowulf's hold was as fierce as ever; yet none the less the two figures **burst** apart – and Grendel with a frightful shriek **staggered** to the doorway and through it, and **fled wailing** into the night …

This could be rewritten as:
*Beowulf's hold was as fierce as ever; yet none the less the two figures **moved** apart – and Grendel with a frightful shriek **ran** to the doorway and through it, and **left complaining** into the night …*

Explain why the first version is better and what the verbs add to the effect of the writing.

(3 marks)

Focus: Comment on the writer's use of language, grammatical and literary features at word and sentence level.

Take each verb separately. Consider what each verb adds to the description. If you 'move' you can do this in any way.
The author has been specific about the movements: what sort of movement is 'staggered' rather than 'walked' or 'hopped' or 'ran'? What accurate detail does it add? What extra information does it give to the reader?

Hint: You can find alternative verbs for your own writing.
Use a thesaurus now but not in the exam!

Some BASICS...

6   Find information in the passage to suggest that Beowulf is a hero.   **(2 marks)**

Focus: Deduce, infer and interpret information and events or ideas from the text.

What do you expect a hero to be? Think about what he looks like, how he behaves, what he does and says.

7   The passage aims to create a picture of a monster. How effective do you think the author has been?
You should write about:
- the use of precise detail
- what he looks like
- how he acts
- the use of language to describe him: for example, the sounds he makes.   **(4 marks)**

Focus: Identify and comment on the writer's purposes and viewpoints, and the effect of the text on the reader.

What do you expect a monster to be like? Note down details right from the start about the monster.
With what is he associated?
What does he do?
How does he react and behave?
What information are we given about how he looks?
Look carefully at the language the author uses – the verbs he uses to describe the noises he makes and the bloodthirsty images.

Test Paper 2: Reading

Extending Your SKILLS...

Reading test 2

Reading and interpreting a passage from *Mermaids and Mastodons* by Richard Carrington

In this passage the author discusses sightings of the Loch Ness Monster.

I come now to one of the most famous and, I regret to say, one of the most suspect, of the creature's many visitations. I refer to the appearance in Scotland in the summer of 1933 of the notorious Loch Ness monster. This alleged sea serpent received greater publicity than any previous representative of the genus. Reported in a small way in the *Northern Chronicle* and the *Inverness Courier* during the summer months, it had become by October a major international sensation. Mr Bertram Mills offered £20,000 to anyone who would deliver the monster alive to his circus, while the New York Zoological Society soon put up £5,000 as a similar inducement. There were articles, lectures, and broadcast talks, and the hotels of Inverness were crammed with representatives not only of the British Press but of such unlikely journals as the *Osaka Moinichi* and the *Tokyo Nichinchi*. One enthusiast even offered, in the columns of the *Glasgow News*, to swim across the loch, 'as a challenge to the monster', and a *Daily Mail* expedition triumphantly found examples of its spoor, which it later transpired had been laid down by some wag with an ashtray made from a dried hippopotamus hoof. Finally in June 1934 the creature reached the pinnacle of its fame with the publication of a 228-page book by Commander Gould entirely devoted to its doings. No one sea serpent had ever received such an honour before.

Although the evidence in Gould's book is most painstakingly compiled, it is also, I am afraid, extremely unconvincing. The only fact to emerge from any of the reports is that a number of black humps were seen floating or moving at

Extending Your SKILLS...

various speeds along the surface of the loch. Their number ranged from one to eight, and the witnesses agreed that they must belong to some large animal moving just out of sight below the water. Some people also claimed to have seen a long serpentine neck and small head emerge from the loch, which turned slowly from side to side as if spying out the land before sinking once more beneath the surface. This was sometimes seen alone and sometimes in association with the mysterious humps described above.

The really classic description, however, is probably that provided by Mr and Mrs G. Spicer who claimed actually to have seen the monster on dry land. On July 22nd 1933 they were motoring round the loch in broad daylight when a most extraordinary animal crossed the road in front of their car. It had a thick body without any sign of legs, and a long neck which undulated up and down 'in the manner of a scenic railway'. The colour of its body was grey, like a dirty elephant or rhinoceros, and it moved in a series of jerks. On the forepart of its back it appeared to be carrying a small lamb, young deer, or other animal of indeterminate species. The head was not observed, but Mr Spicer likened the general effect of this astonishing apparition to a huge snail with a long neck.

Excusably, Mr Spicer's story was at first regarded as a hoax, but it was confirmed in startling fashion by a Mr Arthur Grant of Edinburgh, who some six months later claimed that an animal closely resembling Mr Spicer's had loped across the main road in front of his motor cycle. Despite the fact that this episode occurred at night, the moon was high and he was therefore more fortunate than Mr Spicer in being able to make out the details of the head. This was like that of an eel with large eyes set high up towards the crown. He also observed that the animal had strong front flippers and a rounded tail. It was black, about eighteen feet in length, and moved by arching its back on front and hind flippers alternately.

This description, combined with that of Mr Spicer and of those witnesses who had seen the animal in the water, gives us such a clear and unmistakable picture of one of the Phocidae, or true seals, that it seems almost impossible that the 'Loch Ness monster' could have deceived the public for so long. This seal, probably a large specimen of the common seal, *Phoca vitulina*, must have entered the loch by way of the River Ness sometime in the spring of 1933. After an eventful stay of nearly a year it probably returned to the Firth of Beauly and thence to the open sea by the same route. Admittedly some observers of the monster report it to have been much larger than the usual run of seals, and there are slightly different versions of its colour and shape; in my opinion, however, there is not one of these that cannot be accounted for by tricks of light or faulty estimation of measurements. It is also most probable that some of the reports refer not to the seal at all, but to other mammals such as otters, or even water birds or floating tree trunks, which untrained and expectant witnesses might easily transform into mysterious and sinister forms.

Test Paper 2: Reading

Questions 8–14 are about the *Loch Ness Monster*

---

8 Copy and complete the chart to say what each paragraph is about and how
  it is written.

  (3 marks)

Paragraph	What it is about	Person	Tense	Reason
1				
2				
3				
4				
5				

Focus: Comment on the structure and organisation of texts, grammatical and presentational features
      at text level.

Read the passage carefully; notice the tense and person of the verbs, and the
type of language. The tense of a verb can be past, present or future. A change of
tense is usually made for a reason. Notice where the tense changes, and why.
The person of a verb can be singular or plural: for example, *I, he, we, they*.

---

9 Find and copy information to explain why people offered rewards after the
  sighting of the monster.

  (1 mark)

  Focus: Describe, select and retrieve information and events or ideas from the text. Use quotation and
        reference to the text

The question asks you to quote the evidence, so you should use the actual
words from the passage, and put them in quotation marks.
Quote briefly; use only the words you need.

Hint: You can use a dictionary now, but not in an exam!

---

10 How do you know that the Loch Ness monster had become an 'international
   sensation'?

   (1 mark)

   Focus: Deduce, infer and interpret information and events or ideas from the text.

Extending Your SKILLS...

Look in the first paragraph. What 'international references' are you given?

---

11 Summarise the information you are given about Mr and Mrs Spicer's and
Mr Grant's sightings of the Loch Ness monster. **(3 marks)**

Focus: Describe, select and retrieve information and events or ideas from the text. Use quotation
and reference to the text.

Organise your thoughts in a chart. Charts are a useful way of recording relevant information extracted from a passage. You can produce these as rough work and they can be crossed out before you hand in your answers.

	Mr and Mrs Spicer	Mr Grant
Size		
Shape		
Colour		
Movement		
Head		

---

12 Find and copy the words from paragraph 2 which show that the author
has some admiration for Gould's book, but that he does not believe what it
told him. **(3 marks)**

Focus: Describe, select and retrieve information and events or ideas from the text. Use quotation and
reference to the text.

You need to quote the words. Say how the words give you this impression.

---

13 Look carefully at the use of quotation marks in the following two examples.
Explain the writer's differing purposes in using them. **(3 marks)**

One enthusiast even offered, in the columns of the *Glasgow News*, to swim across the loch, 'as a challenge to the monster'...	It had a thick body without any sign of legs, and a long neck which undulated up and down 'in the manner of a scenic railway'.

Focus: Comment on the writer's use of language, grammatical and literary features at word and
sentence level.

29

Test Paper 2: Reading

Why do authors use quotation marks?
What are the purposes of using them here?
Are the reasons different?
Think about whose words they are and where they would have appeared before they were quoted.

---

14 Comment on the writer's attitude to the Loch Ness monster and how he communicates this in the writing.
You should write about:
- whether he tries to be fair by giving both sides of the argument
- the evidence he uses
- the language he uses which expresses his view
- the way in which he structures his argument to persuade you. **(4 marks)**

Focus: Identify and comment on the writer's purposes and viewpoints, and the effect of the text on the reader.

This question forms a summary of information you should have already collected about the author's interpretation of the material. Make some notes, perhaps using a chart, and then take one point at a time. Write in short sentences and use quotations if you can find them. Make sure you cover all four headings given.

Test Paper 2: Reading

Over to YOU...

Reading test 3
Reading and interpreting *The Kraken* by Alfred Lord Tennyson

The Kraken is a mythical sea-monster. Legend says that it is sleeping under the sea and will emerge on land at the end of the world.

The Kraken

Below the thunders of the upper deep;
Far, far beneath in the abysmal sea,
His ancient, dreamless, uninvaded sleep
The Kraken sleepeth; faintest sunlights flee
About his shadowy sides; above him swell
Huge sponges of millennial growth and height;
And far away into the sickly light,
From many a wondrous grot and secret cell
Unnumber'd and enormous polypi
Winnow with giant arms the slumbering green.
There hath he lain for ages and will lie
Battening upon huge seaworms in his sleep
Until the latter fire shall heat the deep;
Then once by man and angels to be seen,
In roaring he shall rise and on the surface die.

Glossary

abysmal	unfathomable distance (especially in depth), bottomless
battening	growing fat
deep	sea
grot	grotto, cave
polypi	sea anemone with cylindrical body surrounded by tentacles
slumbering	sleeping
winnow	the motion of throwing grain into the air so that the wind can separate the grain from the chaff, which blows away

31

Test Paper 2: Reading

Questions 15–22 are about *The Kraken*

---

15 Select and copy words from the poem to prove that the poet imagines the monster to be at the bottom of the sea. **(1 mark)**

   Focus: Describe, select and retrieve information and events or ideas from the text. Use quotation and reference to the text.

Support your answer by quoting briefly from the poem; use quotation marks.

Hint: Read the poem carefully and look for details.

---

16 What does the word 'thunders' suggest about what it was like in this environment? **(2 marks)**

   Focus: Deduce, infer and interpret information and events or ideas from the text.

Think about your senses and read the word to yourself. To which sense does the word appeal? With what do you normally associate the word? What feelings or impression does it give you?

---

17 Suggest a reason why the poet should decide to repeat the word 'far' in 'Far, far beneath in the abysmal sea'. **(1 mark)**

   Focus: Comment on the writer's use of language, grammatical and literary features at word and sentence level.

Poets choose words carefully to achieve effects. What message is he trying to create about the sea? The monster is hidden a long way down, so what could be a good way of communicating this to the reader?

---

18 The poet shows us a world of movement and life surrounding this sleeping monster. Find and copy two pieces of evidence to support this. **(2 marks)**

   Focus: Describe, select and retrieve information and events or ideas from the text. Use quotation and reference to the text.

32

Over to YOU...

Describe the atmosphere in the early part of the poem, which is quiet and without much movement. You need to quote any details which show movement. Look for verbs – action words.

Hint: Remember to use quotation marks.

---

19 What do the adjectives 'shadowy' and 'sickly' add to the effective description of the atmosphere under the sea in the following lines? **(2 marks)**

> ... faintest sunlights flee / About his shadowy sides ...
>
> And far away into the sickly light ...

Focus: Comment on the writer's use of language, grammatical and literary features at word and sentence level.

When you are asked to explain the effectiveness of something, the following expressions might help:
The author is trying to give an impression of …
To do this he uses words such as …
The words … make me think of …
The verb … suggests… The noun … suggests… The adjective … suggests…
The adverb … suggests …

---

20 The following lines describe the movements of undersea creatures. What impressions are created by the metaphors in them? **(3 marks)**

> Unnumber'd and enormous polypi / Winnow with giant arms the slumbering green.

Focus: Comment on the writer's use of language, grammatical and literary features at word and sentence level.

Hint: Metaphors are similar to comparisons but they don't use words such as 'like' and 'as'. They say something **is** something else.

First identify the metaphors ('winnow', 'slumbering'). Ask yourself, can the creatures really 'winnow'? What is the real meaning? What do the two have in common? The writer has deliberately chosen the image because he wants to create that impression. What happens when you 'winnow'? How is it like the movement of the tentacles?

Test Paper 2: Reading

---

21 The poem ends deliberately with a sound – 'roaring' – but the rest of the poem has given an impression of quietness. Why should this be? **(2 marks)**

Focus: Identify and comment on the writer's purposes and viewpoints, and the effect of the text on the reader.

Think about what impression the poet wants to create of the monster.
Why should he suddenly want him to wake up?
What would the consequences of this be?
How does this change your attitude to the creature in comparison to the rest of the poem?

Hint: Look at the introduction to the poem above.

---

22 The poet aims to create a mysterious atmosphere of a sleeping monster which will one day awake and destroy the world. How successful is he in this?
You could write about:
* how he creates a quiet world
* how he creates a luxurious, dark, mysterious world
* how he suggests the monster's future destructive role
* how the language and the effects he uses create this impression. **(2 marks)**

Focus: Identify and comment on the writer's purposes and viewpoints, and the effect of the text on the reader.

Again, much of the material for this final question will have been collected before: for example, images of a quiet world; images of a dark, mysterious world; some of the effect he has created; and the words he has used.
You need to think more carefully about the monster.
What is the legend?
What will happen when it awakes?
How do you feel about this?
What is the poet trying to make you understand about this in the poem?

| Test Paper 2: Writing

Writing test

These two writing assignments are linked to the theme of 'Monsters'.

Major task

- You should spend about 40 minutes on this.
- There are 30 marks available.

Imagine that a scientific experiment goes wrong and that a tiny creature such as an ant becomes enormous. Write about what happens.

Think about these points:
- the creature when it is large, not on how it becomes large
- what it will look like
- what it will look like to us, many times smaller than the creature
- planning the work – not just sight, but hearing, smell, touch and taste
- an effective ending (not 'and then I woke up …').

Planning

- Before you start writing, use the format on this page to help you to plan and write notes.
- Allow time to read your work and check your use of language before you finish.

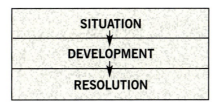

Details of how it looks	Details of how it behaves Does it mean to be evil? Does it understand what has happened to it?
Details of how others react to it	How it could end

35

Test Paper 2: Writing

Minor task

- You should spend about 25 minutes on this.
- There are 20 marks available.

You are a newspaper reporter in the 1930s. The Loch Ness monster has appeared. Write an article about the sightings.

Think about these points:
- interviewing the people who have seen it
- the characters and detail in the passage
- whether you think it is real or not
- the different theories.

Planning

- Before you start writing, use the format on this page to help you to plan and write notes. You do not need to use all the suggested ideas.
- Allow time to read your work and check your use of language and punctuation before you finish.

Headline	Opening paragraphs Who? What? Where? How? When? Why?
Body of the article Details Circumstances of the event People concerned	Sources of information Interviews Quotations Reported speech
Other interpretations Views of others What kind of stir has this caused in the area?	Conclusion Your view

36

Test Paper 3: Reading

Times of celebration

Some BASICS...

This section of the paper is a test of reading and interpretation, although *how* you communicate information is important. The theme linking these three reading texts is 'Times of celebration'.

- You have 1 hour and 15 minutes to answer the questions on the three passages.
- You are given 15 minutes' reading time before this.

Reading test 1

Reading and interpreting a passage from *Life and Literacy* by P J McGeeney

Christmas

There is magic in the Festival of Christmas; more perhaps than we realise. The customs surrounding mistletoe, holly, candles, presents and blazing Yule logs all have their origin in the very distant past when, without a belief in magic and superstition, it would have been difficult to survive.

Among primitive farming peoples, winter, particularly for the poor, was definitely wintry. Clothed in rough and ragged garments, shivering in smoke-filled hovels with only a rushlight to hold back the darkness, and hungry because the remains of the harvest were slowly dwindling, they needed some sort of feast or celebration to welcome the half-way mark towards summer. It was, however, more than an occasion to satisfy the belly. Their livelihood depended upon the rhythm and change of the seasons; when the crops failed famine came and people starved. The sun, moon, stars, wind and rain were watched anxiously in fear and reverence, and when the lightning flashed and the thunder cracked they crouched in terror of the anger of the gods. Out of this grew a religion of sun-worship, a ritual magic consisting of songs, dances, feasts and ceremonies appropriate to the time of the year.

The decorating of buildings with evergreens was done in the belief that it would speed the foliage of spring. Among the Celts, each tree and plant was supposed to have its own magic, the male holly and the female ivy being used in fertility rites. The mistletoe, believed to be a most powerful charm, was cut by Celtic Druids with golden sickles from their sacred oaks. In one form of kissing ceremony, the man had to remove a berry for each kiss, a sacred ritual that was thought to increase and multiply his family and crops.

Fires, candles and lamps were lit because people believed it would strengthen the sun. Originally, the huge Yule log was ceremoniously brought

37

Test Paper 3: Reading

home on Christmas Eve. Sometimes it was sprinkled with corn and cider; sometimes the health of a young girl would be drunk as she sat enthroned upon it. Even today in Sweden, the household is woken by a young girl with a crown of candles blazing on her head. The logs and candles must be kindled with a brand saved from the year before – the New Year arising from the Old.

The extravagant spending and feasting were part of the magic intended to bring luck in the New Year, 'plenty of money and nothing to fear'. The Christmas dinner was the greatest meal of the year. Boar's head was the main dish in the great houses, and often appeared with its mouth propped open on an apple in memory of the days when it was eaten for communion with the 'golden bristled sun-boar', the brute that rode as a golden crest on the helmets of Anglo-Saxon warriors. Plum pudding was originally a runny plum porridge – hence the stirring. In all the odd customs surviving today, the money in the pudding, the holly sprig, the flaming brandy and the luck in mince pies, we have evidence of pagan ritual in the days when each plant, animal and dish had its own peculiar magic or its deeper religious significance in the worship of the sun-god who gave life, and warmth and light.

In the Roman calendar, the shortest day was believed to be December 25th, a happy day when, after months of increasing cold and darkness, the tide turned and the sun began again to have a victory. This feast day of the worshippers of the sun-god, Baal, fell between two other more popular revels which together made the season one of almost continuous junketing.

Some BASICS...

First, there was the Festival of the Saturnalia, which was held from the 17th to 23rd of December. For a few days the social order was turned topsy-turvy: the humble were allowed to lord it over their betters. A special feature was the election by the people of a mad king, the Lord of Misrule, a good-hearted tyrant whose word was law among the revellers. He could command whatever he wished. Someone would be told to shout that he was a fool; another to dance naked in the streets; and another to carry a fat matron three times round the square. The rich man was instructed to 'feast his slaves and let his friends serve with him'. Laws were laid down for the proper observance of the festival:

'All business, public or private, is forbidden during the feast days, except that which contributes to sport and revelry. Let no one work except cooks and bakers. All men shall be equal, free and slave, rich and poor. Anger and threats are against the law.'

Second, there was the New Year feast of the Calends which began on 1st January and lasted for several days. Like the Saturnalia, it was an occasion for men to let themselves go.

In the Middle Ages, this strange mixture of pagan magic was given added light and loveliness by the Christian legend of the Nativity, with its rich appealing imagery of stars and shepherds, wise men and cattle, and mother and child. The setting out of the Crib and the acting of the Nativity Play were used to illustrate the story to people who could not read or write. Later there developed the carols, the best of which were written in the 14th to the 16th centuries.

As time passed, though ancient customs remained, their meaning was gradually forgotten and new customs emerged. The Feast of Stephen became known as Boxing Day, named supposedly from the boxes in which apprentices collected money from their master's customers. To the innumerable dishes on the table turkey was added when it was introduced from Mexico in the 16th century. Queen Victoria's husband, Prince Albert, no doubt remembering his childhood in Germany, had a fine tree set up at Windsor in 1841. Loyal subjects, always eager to imitate royalty, quickly copied him and, together with another German custom, the Christmas stocking, it soon became widespread. It was in 1843 that someone sent the first Christmas card. He would have been amazed to know that he had begun a vast post office operation of carting, year by year, acres of cardboard tonnage depicting robins, stage coaches and fine old English gentlemen.

Test Paper 3: Reading

Questions 1–8 are about *Christmas*

---

1   Find and copy three details from the text which explain why 'primitive farming peoples' needed a mid-winter celebration.   **(1 mark)**

Focus: Describe, select and retrieve information and events or ideas from the text. Use quotation and reference to the text.

You will need to quote the actual words as the question asks you to 'find and copy'. The information is in the second paragraph.

---

2   Explain why these people watched natural phenomena so intently.   **(1 mark)**

Focus: Deduce, infer and interpret information and events or ideas from the text.

First decide what the 'phenomena' could be. The passage tells you why these were important to people and with what they believed they were connected.

---

3   Copy and complete the following chart to summarise what the passage tells you about the origins of Christmas traditions.   **(3 marks)**

Tradition	Origin
Decorating with evergreens	
Candles	
Christmas dinner	
The Crib	
Boxing Day	
Christmas trees	

Focus: Describe, select and retrieve information and events or ideas from the text. Use quotation and reference to the text.

The information for this answer can be found throughout the passage. In questions like this in the exam, underline the relevant sections (perhaps in a different colour). Use your own words to complete the chart.

40

Some BASICS...

4   Match each of the first five paragraphs to its subject.   (3 marks)

Paragraph 1		The need for celebration
Paragraph 2		The use of light and fire as symbols
Paragraph 3		The connection between Christmas and old traditions
Paragraph 4		The inspiration for food
Paragraph 5		The use of natural vegetation as a symbol

Focus: Comment on the structure and organisation of texts, grammatical and presentational features at text level.

Skim-read the first five paragraphs again. Note what each of them is really about – not all the detail which is reinforcing the subject matter.

5   Explain in your own words what happened during Saturnalia and how it came to be incorporated into the celebration of Christmas.   (2 marks)

Focus: Deduce, infer and interpret information and events or ideas from the text.

Note that the question asks for your own words, so it is testing if you understand some of the difficult words and can write sentences to explain these things to your reader. For this exercise you can use a dictionary, but not in the exam. Write in short sentences. Take the explanation one step at a time.

6   How did the concept of a winter celebration change after the Middle Ages?
                                                                              (1 mark)

Focus: Describe, select and retrieve information and events or ideas from the text. Use quotation and reference to the text.

There is only one mark for this question so only a short answer is expected. Use your own words because you are not asked to 'copy'.

41

Test Paper 3: Reading

---

7   The writer uses italics and quotation marks for the following piece of text, as well as setting it out differently. Explain why.   **(2 marks)**

> *'All business, public or private, is forbidden during the feast days, except that which contributes to sport and revelry. Let no one work except cooks and bakers.*
> *All men shall be equal, free and slave, rich and poor. Anger and threats are against the law.'*

Focus: Comment on the writer's use of language, grammatical and literary features at word and sentence level.

This part of the text obviously looks very different and the author will have done this deliberately.

First of all decide what the piece of writing is saying. Why is it different from the rest? Is it a quotation? If so, from where?

---

8   In the passage the author aims to inform the reader in an accurate and entertaining way. How successful is he in doing this?
You should write about:
- the author's use of examples and how you enjoyed them
- the author's tone of voice and his use of humour
- the structure of the passage (is it chronological or non-chronological?).   **(3 marks)**

Focus: Identify and comment on the writer's purposes and viewpoints, and the effect of the text on the reader.

Much of this answer comes from the answers you have already written.
First of all: what is the aim of an explanation?
Which parts are amusing? Is this because of the examples used or the way in which the author talks about them (his tone)?
The structure of the passage is important. Draw some conclusions about this and comment on how important this can be in an explanation.

Test Paper 3: Reading

Extending Your SKILLS...

Reading test 2
Reading and interpreting a passage from *Plot Night* by William Mayne

This passage is about the adventures of a gang on November 5th – Bonfire Night.

L for Leader went in front, carrying the guy. Behind her walked Andy, and then John. Amy stayed at the back of the line.

Then there was no more talking, because a Roman candle was shooting up its fire and bursting it overhead.

The banging fireworks were taken to one side of the fire, and a little way off, and the gentle ones, for the smaller children, were lit on the other side, so there were two parties.

'Mothers and kids for the pretty ones,' said Andy. 'And gangs and dads for the loud ones over here.'

At first Amy jumped at all the bangs. Mother asked her whether she would like to go home. But she couldn't go, because she had to see the silver and golden fountains, and the green and red lights. When she saw the fountains she thought they were water. She had once seen real fountains. She wanted to know why the water in the taps at home was plain and not coloured.

The bonfire grew smaller, and its heat grew larger. People had to go further and further away from it. It was like a small sun flaming in the night.

John found Daddy and asked him whether he had brought the big rocket. Daddy said he was keeping it to end the show with. He was wondering what to

43

Test Paper 3: Reading

stand it in. Small rockets could be stood in bottles. But this one was so big that it would pull a bottle over. If it did that it would streak across the ground, and might even get out into the road and attack a bus.

Catherine wheels were the best favourite. They had a bad habit of coming off the pin, but when they worked they lasted longest and changed colour all the time. They had come with a little stick, with a pin all ready in the end of it, so that you could hold it. Amy held one, with her eyes tight closed and her face turned away. After that she even came and asked for a banger to be thrown at her. She stood about a yard away, and jumped into the air when it blew up, and ran back to Mother feeling she was the bravest person there.

Some people shrieked. Sylvia did. Andy said that L for Leader would have shut her up long ago, but tonight they were having no leaders, so he let her carry on.

Mary got by herself, and exploded her fireworks one by one until they were all gone. Then she picked up the bodies and threw them in the fire. One of them was still alive, and spat back a red blob, then a green blob, before wrinkling itself up black in the embers.

Andy shared out his fireworks with Nick's gang, who had used theirs up in the last few days. Now they were hungry for them. They took great care to ask Andy to watch his own bangers being lit and his own rockets being sent into space.

The big rocket had to wait until they were all on the way home. There was nothing to stand it in near the bonfire. The only place in the park was the hollow gatepost beside the lane. It was just right. People had filled it half full of stones and gravel, dropping a piece in now and then over the years to see what happened. Now it was just the right depth to hold the bottom of the stick and leave the part that had to be lit over the side.

John helped Daddy stand the rocket in the right place, so that it would go over the park and not over the houses. Then Daddy touched a flame to the blue paper, and it began to glow.

The little red glow took a long time to work. Then it spat once. It glowed more, coughed out some smoke, and then a long tail of flame. The rocket seemed to stand on the flame for a long time, it wasn't really a long time, but just long enough for you to think it hadn't gone yet.

Then there was a roar, and the rocket had gone. Before it went it had got itself ready, like a runner, and when it did go it was out to break the record. It looked as if it would never stop. It went up in a curve of fire, then thudded softly, and there was nothing to be seen. Then there was a shower of new bright stars in the sky, dropping, dropping, with smoke above them, and fading as they came. Then each one went out, as if it had gone behind something. In the silence that followed, there was a tumbling sound, and the shell of the rocket, and its stick, rattled in the branches of a tree in the park.

Extending Your SKILLS...

Questions 9–16 are about *Plot Night*

---

9   Find and copy two pieces of information from the first two paragraphs
     which tell us that we are at a November 5th celebration.   **(1 mark)**

     Focus: Describe, select and retrieve information and events or ideas from the text. Use quotation
              and reference to the text.

You need to quote. The examiner has asked you to 'find and copy'.

---

10   Select and copy two pieces of evidence to show how Amy reacted to her first
     experience of fireworks. Explain why you have chosen each piece of evidence.
                                                                    (3 marks)

     Focus: Describe, select and retrieve information and events or ideas from the text. Use quotation
              and reference to the text.

The answer to this question will be found in parts of the passage where Amy
features. The evidence should be a quotation and then you need to comment –
perhaps only in a sentence – about what this suggests.

---

11   The passage uses poetic language and devices to describe the fireworks.
     Explain the simile in: 'It was like a small sun flaming in the night.' Comment
     on how effective you think this is as an image for a firework.   **(2 marks)**

     Focus: Comment on the writer's use of language, grammatical and literary features at word
              and sentence level.

Hint: Remember: a simile is a comparison using **like** or **as**.

You need to decide which two things are being compared here. The
characteristics of both things will be important to making the image a
successful one. What are the characteristics of a firework? and of a sun? How
are the two things similar?

45

Test Paper 3: Reading

12 In the following paragraph the author uses a special technique for making the fireworks come alive. What impressions does he create and how does the technique work?

(3 marks)

> Mary got by herself, and exploded her fireworks one by one until they were all gone. Then she picked up the bodies and threw them in the fire. One of them was still alive, and spat back a red blob, then a green blob, before wrinkling itself up black in the embers.

Focus: Comment on the writer's use of language, grammatical and literary features at word and sentence level.

Personification is an important technique, used to make things come alive in descriptions. Decide: what aspects of the fireworks are made human? Are these realistic? Can I imagine them better when they come to life?

13 Explain why the writer chose to repeat a word in the following description. **(1 mark)**

> Then there was a shower of new bright stars in the sky, dropping, dropping, with smoke above them, and fading as they came.

Focus: Identify and comment on the writer's purposes and viewpoints, and the effect of the text on the reader.

Writers choose to repeat words deliberately. Which word is repeated? What is the writer describing? How does saying the word again make the picture in your mind a better one?

14 Write about the difficulties of finding an appropriate place to launch the rocket. Why was the final place they chose a suitable one?

(3 marks)

Focus: Deduce, infer and interpret information and events or ideas from the text.

Find the paragraphs in which the rocket is discussed. Use the detail in the passage and not your own experience. Make brief notes. Work out the best order for the information. Write your explanation in short sentences, using your own words.

46

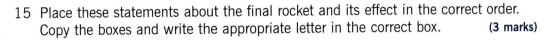

Extending Your SKILLS...

15 Place these statements about the final rocket and its effect in the correct order. Copy the boxes and write the appropriate letter in the correct box. **(3 marks)**

   A. It curved and exploded before disappearing.
   B. The children heard the used rocket dropping in the park.
   C. Once lit, it glowed and made some noise but did not seem to move.
   D. The lights went out and there was silence.
   E. It made a loud noise and went up into the sky.
   F. Then it exploded again into a shower of bright lights which streamed downwards.

1	2	3	4	5	6

Focus: Comment on the structure and organisation of texts, grammatical and presentational features at text level.

Read the last paragraph again. Use a dictionary to look up any words you do not understand. Make a numbered list of the facts given in the paragraph. Match these with the list in the question.

16 What evidence can you find to suggest that this passage is taken from a book meant for younger children?
   You could write about:
   • the use of certain types of sentences
   • the length of the sentences
   • the names of the characters
   • the tone of the passage.   **(3 marks)**

Focus: Identify and comment on the writer's purposes and viewpoints, and the effect of the text on the reader.

Ask yourself: Do young children need shorter or longer sentences? Easier or more difficult words? Find examples of each.
Look at what the characters call their parents. Do adults have gangs led by 'L for Leader'? Who would find a firework display more exciting: children or adults?

47

Test Paper 3: Reading

Over to YOU...

Reading test 3
Reading and interpreting *Diwali in Kerala* by Les Ray

Kerala is a state in south-west India. Diwali is the festival of light celebrated all over the Hindu world. It marks the return of Rama, after having rescued his wife Sita from the King of the Demons, Ravana. He rescued her in Sri Lanka with the help of Hanuman, King of the Monkeys. Hundreds of small clay lamps (divas) are lit in memory of their return – a symbol of light (good) conquering the dark (evil).

Diwali in Kerala

We revel in the silence and fading light over the palms.
The birds in silhouette swoop to gorge upon their final insects, and then
There is a single, pivotal moment of dusk, when darkness carefully unfolds itself
And you can see an emerging trail of tiny, flickering lamps –
Row after row of divas receding into infinity like a mathematical equation.

It is the time of Rama – a celebration.
His faithful Sita belongs to him once more.
Cleverly, the King of the Monkeys and his army have knitted their tails
Across the blockage of ocean to Sri Lanka.
The King of the Demons is dead.
Ravana, the haunter of children's dreams, has gone.
But this is not an end, just the beginning.

Over to YOU...

> Tiny flames are not enough for victory.
> The body of evil must be reduced to dust.
> For just one day the poor take control and
> They explode the weaponry of fireworks,
> Cracking the sky, spreading the small pieces of the Demon King
> Over the skies and dissolving them in a multi-coloured carnage.
>
> The din passes on.
> Flames glimmer and flare
> And illuminate the images of Rama, garlanded and smiling.
>
> He knows that light will always struggle to shine through darkness.
> We feel that too, merging with the people's hope
> As we stand among the fiery remnants –
> Returning to the silence and the faded light.

Questions 17–23 are about *Diwali in Kerala*

17 Find and copy two pieces of information which give the reader a sense of time of day and location. **(2 marks)**

Focus: Describe, select and retrieve information and events or ideas from the text. Use quotation and reference to the text.

Look in the first verse to find this information. You are asked to 'find and copy', so you will need to quote the actual words. Don't forget quotation marks.

18 Explain why the birds are 'in silhouette'. **(1 mark)**

Focus: Deduce, infer and interpret information and events or ideas from the text.

First of all find out the meaning of 'silhouette'.
What does the poet tell you about the time of day?
Would this area have bright street lights?

49

Test Paper 3: Reading

19 According to the legend, the King of the Monkeys helped Rama to cross the sea. From the information given in the poem, outline how you think they did this. **(2 marks)**

Focus: Deduce, infer and interpret information and events or ideas from the text.

Look at what verse 2 tells you about this. What did the army of the King of the Monkeys do? Why was the ocean 'a blockage'?

20 Explain the metaphors in the following two examples. Describe the picture they create in your mind. **(4 marks)**

the weaponry of fireworks

in a multi-coloured carnage

Focus: Comment on the writer's use of language, grammatical and literary features at word and sentence level.

Hint: Remember: metaphors are similar to comparisons but they do not use words such as **like** or **as**.

With metaphors you need to think about what things are being compared and how suitable they are. You may find a chart useful.

Compared to	Characteristics
weaponry	guns, bombs

When you are asked to describe 'the picture they create in your mind' there is no 'right answer' as long as you use the information from the poem, so don't be afraid to explain how you have reacted to the image in the poem.

21 'The body of evil must be reduced to dust.' From the evidence in the poem about the meaning of Diwali, what do the exploding fireworks symbolise? **(1 mark)**

Focus: Deduce, infer and interpret information and events or ideas from the text.

Over to YOU...

Whose 'body' are we talking about in the poem? Which character has been destroyed? Is he an evil or a good character? How will the people show their power over him to show that they have won? How can he be 'turned to dust'?

Hint: Look at the introduction to the poem.

---

22 Explain why the author has pictured Rama smiling. How does this link with the following lines? **(2 marks)**

> But this is not an end, just the beginning.
> He knows that light will always struggle to shine through darkness.

Focus: Deduce, infer and interpret information and events or ideas from the text.

The images are the statues and pictures of the god. What does he know, and others might not, which would make him smile?
Would he be happy that evil has been destroyed?
Think about the images of light and dark. What do they normally mean to people?

---

23 The poet aims to give you an atmospheric description of a festival and its effect on the narrator. How successful has he been?
You could write about:
- the structure of the poem – the atmosphere at the beginning and end
- how this is different from the activity and atmosphere in the main part of the poem
- the imagery of the fireworks
- the way he describes the scene
- what the festival really means to the people watching it. **(3 marks)**

Focus: Identify and comment on the writer's purposes and viewpoints, and the effect of the text on the reader.

Look carefully at the beginning and the end. What words tell you about the level of noise and the atmosphere? How is this different from the central part of the poem?
You have already commented on some of the images to do with the fireworks and what they mean to the people at this time of celebration.
Draw some conclusions from the poem about the meaning of the festival.
Look at the introductory notes; they should help you.

| Test Paper 3: Writing

Writing test

These two writing assignments are linked to the theme of 'Times of celebration'.

Major task

- You should spend about 40 minutes on this.
- There are 30 marks available.

Write an account of the most memorable celebration you can remember.

Think about these points:
- the name of the festival or celebration as your title
- the reason for the festival
- what happens there or at that time of year
- how you were involved
- why this was so special to you.

Planning

- Before you start writing, use the format on this page to help you to plan and write notes.
- Allow time to read your work and check your use of language before you finish.

Title	**History of the festival** When? Where? What? Why?
Key events Make notes Include only important points	**Chronological (time) order of events** Paragraph 1 Paragraph 2 Paragraph 3 Give your reasons why it was so great
Points about the style of a recount Linking words and phrases: As a result of ... However ... Use of past tense	**Conclusion** An evaluation

52

The REAL THING...

Minor task

- You should spend about 25 minutes on this.
- There are 20 marks available.

A friend from overseas is about to visit you. The visit will coincide with a major festival or celebration of which this person has no knowledge or understanding. Write a letter or an e-mail providing some advice about how to prepare for it.

- Write no more than three paragraphs.
- Think about the relevant details only.
- Be careful to explain important things if your friend has no concept of what is involved.

Planning

- Before you start writing, use the format on this page to help you to plan the scene.
- Allow time to read your work and check your use of language and punctuation before you finish.

Sender's details Address or e-mail address, set out correctly Date	Greeting Decide on appropriate tone Friendly? Formal?
Opening State the purpose of writing Make some personal enquiries to be polite	The body of the letter or e-mail Take the points logically and illustrate them with examples Point 1 Point 2 Point 3
The ending This should be linked to the opening Formal or informal?

53

| Test Paper 4: Reading

Woodlands

Some BASICS...

This section of the paper is a test of reading and interpretation, although *how* you communicate information is important. The theme linking these three reading texts is 'Woodlands'.

- You have 1 hour and 15 minutes to answer the questions on the three passages.
- You are given 15 minutes' reading time before this.

Reading test 1
Reading and interpreting a passage from *The Wind in the Willows* by Kenneth Grahame

The cover blurb describes the story as 'a tale of rural life which has enchanted generations of children and adults since it was published in 1908'. In this passage the Mole goes into the Wild Wood.

It was a cold still afternoon with a hard steely sky overhead, when he slipped out of the warm parlour into the open air. The country lay bare and entirely leafless around him, and he thought that he had never seen so far and so intimately into the insides of things as on that winter day when Nature was deep in her annual slumber and seemed to have kicked the clothes off. Copses, dells, quarries and all hidden places, which had been mysterious mines for exploration in leafy summer, now exposed themselves and their secrets pathetically, and seemed to ask him to overlook their shabby poverty for a while, till they could riot in rich masquerade as before, and trick and entice him with the old deceptions. It was pitiful in a way, and yet cheering – even exhilarating. He was glad that he liked the country undecorated, hard, and stripped of its finery. He had got down to the bare bones of it, and they were fine and strong and simple. He did not want the warm clover and the play of seeding grasses; the screens of quickset, the billowy drapery of beech and elm seemed best away; and with great cheerfulness of spirit he pushed on towards the Wild Wood, which lay before him low and threatening, like a black reef in some still southern sea.

   There was nothing to alarm him at first entry. Twigs crackled under his feet, logs tripped him, funguses on stumps resembled caricatures, and startled him for the moment by their likeness to something familiar and far away; but that was all fun, and exciting. It led him on, and he penetrated to where the light was less, and trees crouched nearer and nearer, and holes made ugly mouths at him on either side.

Some BASICS...

Everything was very still now. The dusk advanced on to him steadily, rapidly, gathering in behind and before; and the light seemed to be draining away like flood-water.

Then the faces began.

It was over his shoulder, and indistinctly, that he first thought he saw a face: a little evil wedge-shaped face, looking out at him from a hole. When he turned and confronted it, the thing had vanished.

He quickened his pace, telling himself cheerfully not to begin imagining things, or there would be simply no end to it. He passed another hole, and another, and another; and then – yes! – no! – yes! certainly a little narrow face, with hard eyes, had flashed up for an instant from a hole, and was gone. He hesitated – braced himself up for an effort and strode on. Then suddenly, and as if it had been so all the time, every hole, far and near, and there were hundreds of them, seemed to possess its face, coming and going rapidly, all fixing on him glances of malice and hatred: all hard-eyed and evil and sharp.

If he could only get away from the holes in the banks, he thought, there would be no more faces. He swung off the path and plunged into the untrodden places of the wood.

Then the whistling began.

Very faint and shrill it was, and far behind him, when first he heard it; but somehow it made him hurry forward. Then, still very faint and shrill, it sounded far ahead of him, and made him hesitate and want to go back. As he halted in indecision it broke out on either side, and seemed to be caught up and passed on throughout the whole length of the wood to its furthest limit. They were up and alert and ready, evidently, whoever they were! And he – he was alone, and unarmed, and far from any help; and the night was closing in.

Then the pattering began.

Test Paper 4: Reading

Questions 1–7 are about *The Wind in the Willows*

---

1   Select and copy the words from the first paragraph which show what the
weather was like.   **(1 mark)**

     Focus: Describe, select and retrieve information and events or ideas from the text. Use quotation
and reference to the text.

Notice the words 'select and copy'. You need to find the words and then copy them, using quotation marks.

---

2   Find and copy three phrases which tell you what time of year it was.

     (2 marks)

     Focus: Describe, select and retrieve information and events or ideas from the text. Use quotation
and reference to the text.

Notice the words 'find and copy'. This suggests that the examiner is looking for quotations, and not your own words. If you are given a number of things to find, in this case three, they may not be the only points; there may be others for you to choose from. Give only three.

---

3   What is the purpose of the dashes in the following sentence?

> He passed another hole, and another, and another; and then – yes! – no! –
> yes! certainly a little narrow face, with hard eyes, had flashed up for an
> instant from a hole, and was gone.

- How do the dashes affect the way in which you read the sentence?
- What sort of effect do they create?
- Why does the writer want to create this effect?   **(3 marks)**

Focus: Comment on the writer's use of language, grammatical and literary features at word and
sentence level.

Think about the way in which the Mole felt about the Wild Wood at first.
What changed his feelings?
How does the writer show this change of feelings?

Hint: Read the sentence aloud. You can't do this in an exam, but you can imagine yourself reading it aloud.

56

Some BASICS...

4   Quote two examples of the writer's use of contrast which emphasise the coldness and bareness of the Wild Wood. **(2 marks)**

Focus: Describe, select and retrieve information and events or ideas from the text. Use quotation and reference to the text.

Notice that the question asks you to quote. Here you are looking for 'the writer's use of contrast', so you need to look at the words carefully. Find the part of the passage where he introduces the Wild Wood.

5   How did the Mole feel about the Wild Wood when he first thought about it? **(2 marks)**

Focus: Deduce, infer and interpret information and events or ideas from the text.

Find the part of the passage where the Wild Wood is first mentioned and find the words which show how the Mole approaches it.

6   What is the first suggestion that the Wild Wood is not a pleasant place? **(2 marks)**

Focus: Deduce, infer and interpret information and events or ideas from the text.

Find the part of the passage where the Wild Wood is first mentioned.

7   How does the writer gradually build up the threatening atmosphere of the Wild Wood?
You should write about:
- how the Mole felt at first about things which startled him
- the use of comparisons and metaphors
- the effect of very short sentences following long ones. **(4 marks)**

Focus: Identify and comment on the writer's purposes and viewpoints, and the effect of the text on the reader.

Think about:
- why the writer gives a step-by-step recount of Mole's walk into the Wild Wood
- the rhythm of the Mole's journey – this reflects his feelings
- the things which seem to appear and then disappear in the Wild Wood
- the effect of the three very short paragraphs (each consisting of a single short sentence) which repeat one another in style.

57

Test Paper 4: Reading

Extending Your SKILLS...

Reading test 2
Reading and interpreting a poem by Rudyard Kipling

The Way Through the Woods

They shut the road through the woods
Seventy years ago.
Weather and rain have undone it again,
And now you would never know
There was once a road through the woods
Before they planted the trees.
It is underneath the coppice and heath
And the thin anemones.
Only the keeper sees
That, where the ring-dove broods,
And the badgers roll at ease,
There was once a road through the woods.

Yet, if you enter the woods
Of a summer evening late,
When the night-air cools on the trout-ringed pools
Where the otter whistles his mate
(They fear not men in the woods,
Because they see so few)
You will hear the beat of a horse's feet,
And the swish of a skirt in the dew,
Steadily cantering through
The misty solitudes,
As though they perfectly knew
The old lost road through the woods …
But there is no road through the woods.

Questions 8–15 are about *The Way Through the Woods*

8 Find and copy three examples of animals which live in the woods. **(1 mark)**

Focus: Describe, select and retrieve information and events or ideas from the text. Use quotation and reference to the text.

58

Extending Your SKILLS...

Notice the words 'find and copy'. This suggests that the examiner is looking for quotations, and not your own words. If you are given a number of things to find, in this case three, these may not be the only points; there may be others. Give only three.

---

9 How have the woods changed? Select and copy words to support what you say. **(2 marks)**

Focus: Deduce, infer and interpret information and events or ideas from the text.

Notice the words 'select and copy'. You should find the words and copy them, using quotation marks.

---

10 What is the effect of the phrase 'misty solitudes' in the second verse? **(1 mark)**

Focus: Comment on the writer's use of language, grammatical and literary features at word and sentence level.

Think about the atmosphere of the woods. What kind of atmosphere does the phrase suggest?

---

11 Find two examples of internal rhyme in the second verse. **(2 marks)**

Focus: Comment on the writer's use of language, grammatical and literary features at word and sentence level.

You should make sure you know the meanings of common literary terms such as 'internal rhyme'. Internal rhyme is where rhyme occurs within the same line.

---

12 How does the poet suggest that, although 'you would never know / There was once a road through the woods', the road has not completely disappeared? **(2 marks)**

Focus: Identify and comment on the writer's purposes and viewpoints, and the effect of the text on the reader.

Test Paper 4: Reading

Look for clues that the road could not be completely removed – that it persists, despite the fact that 'they shut the road'.
Look for clues that anyone (or any animal) is aware of the road.

---

13 Which two lines in the first verse create an atmosphere of peace and tranquillity, and how does the poet use alliteration to create this effect? **(3 marks)**

Focus: Identify and comment on the writer's purposes and viewpoints, and the effect of the text on the reader.

Notice the words which describe the animals' behaviour.
Think about the repeated sounds in the words.
Some sounds have a gentler effect than others. Which sound has a gentle, peaceful effect here?

Hint: Alliteration is the repetition of the initial sounds of words to create an effect.

---

14 Describe the atmosphere of the second verse. Which words create this effect?
(3 marks)

Focus: Identify and comment on the writer's purposes and viewpoints, and the effect of the text on the reader.

Think about the literal meaning of the verse.
Notice the effect of alliteration. The alliterated sounds have a mysterious effect (rather than the peaceful, tranquil effect of those in the first verse).

---

15 What is the effect of repetition in the poem?
You should write about:
- repeated words or phrases
- lines with a similar rhythm
- what people's actions achieved
- how effectively they shut the road. **(4 marks)**

Focus: Identify and comment on the writer's purposes and viewpoints, and the effect of the text on the reader.

You should trust your own impressions of the poem – the impressions you have when you read it to yourself and imagine the woods. Think about the way in which the poet has created these impressions.
Write your ideas in your own words but support them with quotations from the poem.

Test Paper 4: Reading

Over to YOU...

Reading test 3
Reading and interpreting a passage adapted from the Woodland Trust website

Britain's rainforests need protecting now

Broadleaved woodland contains more endangered species than any other UK habitat. Fifty per cent of the UK's ancient woodland has been lost since the 1930s and today, only two per cent of total land area is covered by ancient woodland. The report warns that its survival still hangs in the balance as a result of three key factors.

    Looking ahead, changes in the climate, including higher temperatures, changes in rainfall patterns, drought and the frequency of storms, will have a dramatic impact on ancient woodland. A number of the plants and animals which live in ancient woodland are unlikely to be able to respond fast enough to these climate changes and may become scarce or even extinct in the wild. For example, plants such as bluebells, Solomon's seal and wood anemone are particularly at risk. Milder winters may also lead to increasing numbers and varieties of insect pests from home and abroad; while summer droughts can make animals and plants vulnerable to disease.

    A lack of legal protection for woodland is allowing it to be damaged. The Woodland Trust warns that 85 per cent of ancient woodland has no legal protection and that loopholes in the law, and poor planning regulations, are not helping. Finally, intensive agricultural practices are isolating fragments of woodland.

Test Paper 4: Reading

Furthermore, overgrazing by livestock and deer is halting the growth of new trees and preventing ancient woodland from regenerating. In addition to this, many remaining ancient broadleaved woodland sites are fighting to survive in dense canopies of planted conifers.

Ancient woodland is one of our richest habitats for wildlife. Ancient woods are places of great beauty, reservoirs of archaeology and economic history, and a source of inspiration for local culture and folklore – they are effectively Britain's rainforests.

Mike Townsend, the Woodland Trust's Chief Executive, says: "Despite a growing understanding of the value of ancient woodlands and the creation of a number of new policies and programmes for their protection and enhancement, ancient woodland continues to be threatened and destroyed. The immediate challenge for the new century is to translate the promises and new policies of the last 10 years into action and begin to plug the gaps. Ancient woods are a finite resource which can never be replaced; their future survival depends on action now."

To tackle the situation the Woodland Trust is calling for a number of measures to be put into practice immediately, including:

- the creation of a new form of conservation status for important local wildlife sites like ancient woodland
- the creation by the government of formal planning guidance for local authorities to create stronger policies in local plans so that damaging plans can be refused
- government support for renewable and energy-efficient technologies instead of conventional fossil fuel-based plans
- a reform of the Farm Woodland Premium Scheme to ensure that woodland creation on farms is used to buffer ancient woods where possible.

Questions 16–21 are about *Britain's rainforests need protecting now*

16 Find and copy from the second paragraph the four aspects of climate change which affect the survival of Britain's ancient woodland. **(3 marks)**

Focus: Describe, select and retrieve information and events or ideas from the text. Use quotation and reference to the text.

Notice that you are asked to find *the* four aspects of climate change. This tells you that there are only four and that you should find all of them.

Over to YOU...

17 Explain what 'hangs in the balance' means in the first paragraph. **(1 mark)**

   Focus: Comment on the writer's use of language, grammatical and literary features at word and sentence level.

Think about the words and the context in which they are used. You can probably work out what the expression means; or, in class, use a dictionary.

18 Three 'key factors' are mentioned in the report as causing the future of ancient woodlands to 'hang in the balance'. Each factor is the topic of a paragraph. Match each paragraph to its topic. **(2 marks)**

Paragraph	Topic
2	Damage by animals and by other types of trees
3	Changes in climate
4	A lack of legal protection

   Focus: Comment on the structure and organisation of texts, grammatical and presentational features at text level.

Notice the opening sentences of the paragraphs. These 'topic sentences' tell you what the paragraphs are about. Reread the paragraphs about the factors affecting woodlands and notice the 'topic sentences'.

19 Explain why bullets are used in the final paragraph of the report. **(2 marks)**

   Focus: Comment on the structure and organisation of texts, grammatical and presentational features at text level.

Think about the visual effect of bullets. How do they affect the way in which you read the paragraph? What do they separate and emphasise?

Test Paper 4: Reading

20 Copy and complete the table with information from the passage about the effects of different aspects of the 'key factors' (identified in question 18) on ancient woodlands. **(3 marks)**

Key factor	Effects on trees and other plants	Effects on animals
Mild winters		
Droughts		
Intensive farming		
Overgrazing by livestock and deer		
Dense plantations of conifers		

Focus: Describe, select and retrieve information and events or ideas from the text. Use quotation and reference to the text.

Look for precise descriptions of effects. The report is not always precise: for example, when it uses clauses such as 'are not helping'.

21 This passage aims to persuade the government, and anyone who can influence the government, that ancient woodlands need to be protected. How successful is it? You should write about:
- how language is used to appeal to people's feelings about woodlands
- the way in which statements are supported by facts. **(4 marks)**

Focus: Identify and comment on the writer's purposes and viewpoints, and the effect of the text on the reader.

Look for strong, expressive adjectives and verbs. Where you find a statement of fact or opinion, look for evidence which supports it. Do not worry if you cannot find the evidence – it might not be there! If not, this can be considered to be a weakness of the report.

| Test Paper 4: Writing

Writing test
These two writing assignments are linked to the theme of 'Woodlands'.

Major task
- You should spend about 40 minutes on this.
- There are 30 marks available.

Write a poem about a wood which is endangered and which you want to save.

Think about these points:
- what the wood is like
- what is endangering it
- the message you want to communicate
- the structure of your poem. Think about the way in which you will split it into verses. (It could consist of one long verse and it need not rhyme.) Think about the effect you want to create and the effects of different structures. You could give the poem an interesting shape.
- nouns, adjectives and verbs which will create the effects you want: for example, you might want to appeal to people's emotions about woodlands or you might want to express sadness or anger that nothing is being done to save the wood
- literary devices which you could use: for example, alliteration, onomatopoeia, comparison, simile and metaphor.

Planning
- Before you start writing, use the format on this page to help you to plan and write notes.
- Allow time to read your work and check your use of language before you finish.

The message I want to communicate	The effect I want to create
Useful nouns	Useful verbs	Useful adjectives
Literary devices, and examples of them		

Test Paper 4: Writing

Minor task

- You should spend about 25 minutes on this.
- There are 20 marks available.

Write a postcard from the Mole in *The Wind in the Willows* to another character (for example, the Rat or the Badger) telling him or her about his experiences in the Wild Wood.

You should write a short message which will fit on one side of a postcard.

Think about these points:
- the important things you (the Mole) saw, heard and felt
- what you hope will happen soon.

Reread the passage from *The Wind in the Willows*. Your answers to questions 1–7 will help.

Planning

- Before you start writing, use the format on this page to help you to plan and write notes.
- Do not write your name and address on the postcard, or the address of the character to whom you are writing.
- Allow time to read your work and check your use of language before you finish.

How will you begin the postcard? What tone should it have? Formal or informal?	**The main points** What are the main things you want to write about?
Verbs for what you did and what happened Try to use verbs which are not in the passage (you could use synonyms for some of them if they are appropriate)	**Adjectives to describe the Wild Wood** Use strong adjectives
**Ending the postcard** You are writing to a close friend and so you do not need a formal ending such as 'Yours faithfully', or even 'Yours sincerely', but an informal signing-off word	

| Test Paper 5: Reading

Football

Some BASICS...

This section of the paper is a test of reading and interpretation, although *how* you communicate information is important. The theme linking these three reading texts is 'Football'.

- You have 1 hour and 15 minutes to answer the questions on the three passages.
- You are given 15 minutes' reading time before this.

Reading test 1

Reading and interpreting a passage from *A Legend in his Own Time*

This passage was written by Joe Mercer, who was then manager of Manchester City Football Club. It is from a collection of biographical tributes compiled when Bill Shankly retired as manager of Liverpool Football Club in 1974.

I once thought about writing a book called *The Thoughts of Bill*. But where do you start and where do you finish? There's so much to tell, all the stories through the years. And how could you edit such a book? It would be like trying to condense an encyclopedia into a football programme.

67

Test Paper 5: Reading

There are so many myths about Bill. They say he's tough, he's hard, he's ruthless. Rubbish – he's got a heart of gold, he loves the game, he loves his fans, he loves his players. He's like an old Collie dog: he doesn't like hurting his sheep. He'll drive them, certainly, but bite them – never.

And this is why, since Bill went to Liverpool, they've always been the side you try hardest to beat – the side above all others over whom victory is sweetest.

Bill has built great sides, of course, teams which have been a pleasure to watch as they surged forward and back like waves on the seashore. They were always uncomplicated. That's why they've been so consistent; sides which always did the simple things, the fundamental things, and did them so well. They have belief in one another, a belief which was the most amazing thing imaginable until you remember that Bill gave them something special.

If there is one word to describe Bill it must be 'colossus'. For that is what he has been in the game and throughout his life. He's so basically honest, with a one-track mind for football. And he believes in people. He must be the greatest inspirer in the game. No matter what club he was with they didn't have a bad player in his side – according to him.

He had great qualities as a player, too. He was from the same mould which produced Emlyn Hughes – superbly fit, didn't know when he was licked, a good tackler, a brave player, straightforward, tough and with infectious enthusiasm.

Shankly's presence in the game was a wonderful thing for football. But he was an even more marvellous happening for Liverpool. From the time he arrived there's been only one way – up. And this endless success was mirrored in that amazing relationship with the Kop [the terrace behind the goal at one end of the ground (for home supporters) – now replaced with seating].

When he was at Anfield he was the City of Liverpool's answer to vandalism and hooliganism, because the kids came to see Liverpool. They came to see those red shirts and Shankly was their man, their hero, their football god. He belongs to the Kop. He's one of them. If he hadn't managed Liverpool I'm sure he'd have been on the Kop, dressed in red, singing and chanting "Liverpool, Liverpool."

Bill Shankly is badly missed in football. We need him with us in the game. But I can understand why he retired. I suffered ill health because of the pressures of modern football: training, travelling 200 miles on a scouting trip, arguing with directors and so much more.

And he's wise to get out while he's still fit.

Yes, I'm sure the years must have taken their toll. The nervous energy he used in building Liverpool into the side they became would have lit up the city for years if it could have been turned into electricity.

But of course, he did light up the city and the game.

The sunshine he brought into the game will be remembered for years and the blazing torch of his concept of football will be carried on for many years as his players, in management, preach his testament.

Some BASICS...

Questions 1–7 are about *A Legend in his Own Time*

1   The writer said that there were myths about Bill Shankly. Select and copy the three personal qualities which he called 'myths'. **(1 mark)**

Focus: Describe, select and retrieve information and events or ideas from the text. Use quotation and reference to the text.

You are asked to find *the* three personal qualities – this means that the writer gives only three. Quote from the text, using quotations marks.

2   With what did the writer compare Bill Shankly in the second paragraph, and for what two reasons? **(2 marks)**

Focus: Comment on the writer's use of language, grammatical and literary features at word and sentence level.

Hint: Comparisons usually contain a word such as **like** or **as**.

You are asked to look for two reasons, and so you should find both of them.

3   Find two other comparisons in the passage, and copy and complete the chart. Comment on the impression produced by the comparison. **(3 marks)**

The thing, person or place compared	What he, she or it is compared with	The impression created

Focus: Comment on the writer's use of language, grammatical and literary features at word and sentence level.

Remember, in a comparison the characteristics of both things being compared are important in making the image a successful one.

69

Test Paper 5: Reading

4   What, according to the writer, was the most important thing Bill Shankly did to make Liverpool a top-class football team? **(2 marks)**

Focus: Deduce, infer and interpret information and events or ideas from the text.

Look for what the writer says made the teams do well and which made them difficult to beat.

5   List three qualities which made Bill Shankly a great player when he was a footballer. Select and quote from the passage. **(2 marks)**

Focus: Describe, select and retrieve information and events or ideas from the text. Use quotation and reference to the text.

Read the opening sentence or 'topic sentence' of each paragraph to find out what it is about. Look for the paragraph which is about Bill Shankly as a player.

6   Look for a metaphor near the end of the passage and describe the impression it creates of Bill Shankly. **(2 marks)**

Focus: Comment on the writer's use of language, grammatical and literary features at word and sentence level.

A metaphor compares a person or thing with something else but it does not use words such as 'like', 'as' or 'than'. It is as if the person or thing *is* something else.

7   The writer aims to create a picture of someone special in the world of football. How successful is it?
    You should write about: **(4 marks)**
    - the ways in which the writer comments on Bill Shankly's personal qualities and skill as a manager
    - the ways in which he communicates Bill Shankly's effect on other people.

Focus: Identify and comment on the writer's purposes and viewpoints, and the effect of the text on the reader.

Some of your answers to earlier questions might help you. Look for emphasis, metaphors, comparisons and superlatives.

Test Paper 5: Reading

Extending Your SKILLS...

Reading test 2
Reading and interpreting a poem by Pam Gidney

The humour in this poem comes from puns and plays on words.

A Perfect Match

We met in Nottingham Forest,
    My sweet Airdrie and I.
She smiled and said, 'Alloa!' to me –
    Oh, never say goodbye!

I asked her, 'Is your Motherwell?'
    And she replied, 'I fear
She's got the Academicals
    From drinking too much beer.'

We sat down on a Meadowbank
    And of my love I spoke.
'Queen of the South,' I said to her,
    'My fires of love you Stoke!'

We went to Sheffield, Wednesday.
    Our Hearts were one. Said she:
'Let's wed in Accrington, Stanley,
    Then we'll United be.'

The ring was Stirling silver,
    Our friends, Forfar and wide,
A motley Crewe, all gathered there
    and fought to kiss the bride.

The best man had an awful lisp.
    'Come Raith your glatheth up,'
He said, and each man raised on high
    His Coca-Cola cup.

The honeymoon was spent abroad:
    We flew out east by Ayr,
And found the far-off Orient
    Partick-ularly fair.

We're home, in our own Villa now,
    (The Walsall painted grey)
And on our Chesterfield we sit
    And watch Match of the Day.

Test Paper 5: Reading

Questions 8–14 are about *A Perfect Match*

---

8   This is a narrative poem. How can you tell?   **(2 marks)**

Focus: Comment on the structure and organisation of texts, grammatical and presentational features at text level.

Notice the tense of the verbs and the chronological recount of events.

---

9   How is the love story linked with football throughout the poem?   **(2 marks)**

Focus: Comment on the structure and organisation of texts, grammatical and presentational features at text level.

Look for words connected with football which are used in humorous ways and with new meanings.

---

10   Copy and complete the chart to show six other football clubs which are mentioned in the poem and explain the puns on their names.   **(3 marks)**

Name of football club	Similar sounding word or words with a different meaning
Alloa	Hello

Focus: Comment on the writer's use of language, grammatical and literary features at word and sentence level.

You do not need to know a lot about football to be able to answer this question. The answers are in the poem. Look for the words beginning with capital letters. Look for any names of football teams which you recognise.

Hint: A pun is a humorous use of a word which can have more than one meaning. In a pun the original word can be changed slightly, but not so much that it is not recognisable.

Extending Your SKILLS...

---

11 In verse 2, 'Academicals' refers to the Scottish football club Hamilton Academicals. The play on words here is not obvious; 'Academicals' is probably used as a slang or nonsense word for what? **(2 marks)**

Focus: Comment on the writer's use of language, grammatical and literary features at word and sentence level.

Think about why the mother has 'the Academicals' and what other slang word people might use instead.

---

12 Chesterfield is a football club. Reread verse 8. Why should people sit on a Chesterfield? **(2 marks)**

Focus: Deduce, infer and interpret information and events or ideas from the text.

This question tests your vocabulary. Use a dictionary. In an exam you cannot use a dictionary, but you can work out the meanings of words from their context.

---

13 Comment on the rhythm of the poem and how this suits its tone. **(3 marks)**

Focus: Comment on the structure and organisation of texts, grammatical and presentational features at text level.

Is the rhythm fast or slow, stately or lively? *Tone* means the 'feel' of the poem and how the reader is meant to react to it. Your answers to the earlier questions will help you to come to a decision about the tone of the poem.

---

14 The poem is meant to be funny. How successful is it?
You should write about:
- whether it made you laugh and, if so, which parts of it
- whether readers need to know a lot about football in order to find it funny
- whether the puns are recognisable. **(4 marks)**

Focus: Identify and comment on the writer's purposes and viewpoints, and the effect of the text on the reader.

This question summarises much of what you have already noticed about the poem. Make some notes. Write in your own words but use quotations (in quotation marks) if you find this useful. Support your opinions by quoting from the poem.

73

Test Paper 5: Reading

Reading test 3
Reading and interpreting *Magpies come from behind to beat Charlton* by Paul Fraser

This football report is from the Northeast Echo, *a local newspaper which presents many of its reports on a website of newspapers in the northeast of England.*

Magpies come from behind to beat Charlton
By Paul Fraser

Sir Bobby Robson was given the perfect pick-me-up at St. James' Park on Saturday – three points.

Newcastle United boss Robson had to watch the entire 2-1 victory over Charlton Athletic from the stands, as he recovers from a bad fall at his home on Thursday which left him with a bad back and bruised ribs. But the 69-year-old, still in pain after the match, was given a nice boost when he realised that rapidly rising Newcastle have the title contenders back in their sights. The hard-earned win over Charlton lifted the Magpies to within three points of a Champions' League place with a game in hand.

And that is sweet music to the ears of all Newcastle fans who witnessed the disappointing start to the campaign, which saw them hit bottom spot early on. What will please the Geordie* faithful the most, though, is the way in which they have picked themselves up from their depressing slump.

Only Blackburn Rovers have claimed victory over Newcastle in the Premiership since their impressive derby day success over Sunderland in September and Saturday was their third top-flight win at home on the bounce. Couple that with a rejuvenated European adventure following last Wednesday's memorable 1-0 win over Italian giants Juventus and it is easy to see why spirits are high again around St. James' Park.

What made the weekend's result more pleasing for boss Robson was that the points were assured without four attacking players: Kieron Dyer, Craig Bellamy, Carl Cort and Lomana LuaLua. But gangly forward Shola Ameobi and creative midfielder Jermaine Jenas came in and held their own with two encouraging displays.

And Robson said, "Shola's performance was very important for us. You have got to remember that he is still just a kid. I had no worries about putting him in there with Alan Shearer. I knew he would do us a job, he normally does.

"We had four strikers out on Saturday, four. That's going to be a miss for any team. But I thought we did well and caused them problems."

Robson needs performances from Ameobi and Co if Newcastle are going to come out of the Bellamy injury period unscathed.

Over to YOU...

The talented Welshman flies out to the United States this morning (Monday) to see knee specialist Dr Richard Steadman. It is feared he could face another lengthy spell on the sidelines and if that is the case then Robson's other striking options have to be ready to perform.

Striker LuaLua missed out on Saturday as well with a knee injury and that allowed Ameobi to stake his claim, with promising teenager Michael Chopra named on the bench for the first time in his career. Chopra never entered the field of play but Ameobi did and he could have scored on his first start since the Leeds United clash and only his second of the season.

However, impressive Charlton 'keeper Dean Kiely made a superb save to deny the 21-year-old only his fourth Premiership goal in the second period after the front-man jinked his way past four players. Ameobi and Shearer did make life difficult for Charlton's three-man defence – Richard Rufus, Gary Rowett and Mark Fish – but victory was assured from other sources – most notably Laurent Robert.

The signs were there early on that the left-winger was going to have a productive day, as he was at the centre of nearly all of Newcastle's attacking play. The Frenchman had a long-range shot tipped over; an effort wide; and he fashioned openings for both Jenas and Speed, who both should have put Newcastle in front. Instead, it was Charlton who took the lead after half an hour when Andy O'Brien – making his 50th top-flight appearance in a black and white shirt – failed to head clear a John Robinson centre.

Test Paper 5: Reading

O'Brien's knock fell in between Titus Bramble and Shaun Bartlett and it was the latter who reacted first to go in on goal and fire past Shay Given. It was certainly not what Bramble, who kept his place despite the return from suspension of Nikos Dabizas, deserved as he enjoyed another confident display at the back.

And Robson said, "Where's the boo boys now? They are in their pints somewhere. Titus did well again for us today."

Charlton, who had their shorts stolen before the match, were robbed of the lead seven minutes after taking it, when Andy Griffin continued his rise to hero status on Tyneside. Shearer rolled the ball to the on-rushing Griffin, who from 18 yards struck a sweet right foot shot that powered into Kiely's top corner. If there was a doubt over whether it was Griffin's goal against Juventus, there was no doubt about this one.

Newcastle were on top for the majority of the second half and Kiely had to be alert to save a low Robert drive nine minutes after the restart. But five minutes later the Irish goalkeeper could do nothing about the £10m man's left-foot bullet that flew in after some neat link-up play between Solano, Shearer and Ameobi.

Charlton had their chances to equalise but Newcastle and 'keeper Given stood firm and now they will be hoping for a similar result against Kiev on Tuesday night.

Result: Newcastle 2 – 1 Charlton.

*Geordie – (adjective) from Newcastle upon Tyne or its surrounding area

Questions 15–22 are about *Magpies come from behind to beat Charlton*

15 Name another football team, apart from Charlton, which Newcastle had recently beaten, and one which defeated them.

(1 mark)

Focus: Describe, select and retrieve information and events or ideas from the text. Use quotation and reference to the text.

Skim-read the passage; look out for the names of football clubs and then read the sentences in which they occur. If necessary reread the entire paragraph in which you found the name and the sentence in order to check that you have the correct information.

Over to YOU...

16 If you did not know that the nickname of Newcastle United was 'the Magpies' and that their home ground was St James' Park, how could you find these out from the passage? Select and copy words from the passage which tell you about each of these. **(1 mark)**

Focus: Describe, select and retrieve information and events or ideas from the text. Use quotation and reference to the text.

The words 'select and copy' tell you that you should copy the relevant words from the passage, using quotation marks.

Hint: Reread paragraphs 1, 2 and 4. Also look at the title for a clue.

17 Name as many as you can of the players who were in the Newcastle United and Charlton Athletic teams for the match reported in the passage. Do not name players from any memories you might have of the match; select and copy the names only of players mentioned in the passage. Not all the players might be named. Copy and complete the chart. **(3 marks)**

Newcastle United	Charlton Athletic

Focus: Describe, select and retrieve information and events or ideas from the text. Use quotation and reference to the text.

You should use only information from the passage and not your own knowledge of the football clubs. When you select and copy the names of players you need to read the sentence and probably the paragraph in which they are mentioned to check for which team they were playing.

Test Paper 5: Reading

18 Which players scored Newcastle United's two goals and who scored Charlton Athletic's goal? **(2 marks)**

Focus: Describe, select and retrieve information and events or ideas from the text. Use quotation and reference to the text.

Skim-read the passage, looking out for references to goals and then reading the sentences in which they occur. If necessary read the entire paragraph in which you found the name and the sentence in order to check that you have the correct information.

19 The reporter suggests that Newcastle United made a disappointing start to the season. Select and quote three phrases from paragraph 3 which tell you this. **(1 mark)**

Focus: Deduce, infer and interpret information and events or ideas from the text.

You are asked to select and quote three phrases. Do not quote sentences or clauses or single words. A phrase is a group of words which does not contain a verb.

Hint: Remember to use quotation marks.

20 What facts does the passage give about the Newcastle United player whose family name is Robert? Copy and complete the fact-file. **(2 marks)**

Facts about Robert		The words which tell me this
Personal name		
Nationality		
Playing position		
Transfer fee to Newcastle		

Focus: Describe, select and retrieve information and events or ideas from the text. Use quotation and reference to the text.

Over to YOU...

21 What does 'on the bench' mean in paragraph 10? **(2 marks)**

Focus: Comment on the writer's use of language, grammatical and literary features at word and sentence level.

This tests your vocabulary. You can answer this without using a dictionary. You know what a bench is and can work out why a footballer might be sitting on a bench rather than being on the pitch and how this is different from not being named in the team.

22 To what extent does the report communicate the excitement of the match? You should:
- comment on the pace of the text (is it fast, breathless, slow, measured, restrained?)
- comment on the way in which the lengths of sentences contribute to this effect
- select words which suggest excitement or, if you think the writer could have used more exciting vocabulary, select words which could have been substituted for more exciting ones
- comment on the punctuation. **(4 marks)**

Focus: Identify and comment on the writer's purposes and viewpoints, and the effect of the text on the reader.

You should look for short sentences or clauses which give a feeling of speed and create a fast, exciting pace. Notice the punctuation of the passage: exclamation marks communicate excitement and surprise.

Hint: Notice the language: superlatives and exclamations can create a feeling of excitement.

Test Paper 5: Writing

Writing test

These two writing assignments are linked to the theme of 'Football'.

Major task

- You should spend about 40 minutes on this.
- There are 30 marks available.

Write an argument about whether football matches should be shown only on television channels for which people have to pay.

Think about these points:
- a way in which to introduce the argument so that your view is clear
- the reasons why people should have to pay to watch football on television (even if you do not agree with this)
- the reasons against paying
- supporting the reasons with information, 'research' or 'quotations' (which you can make up)
- summarising the argument, perhaps repeating the view you expressed at the beginning
- writing in the present tense.

Planning

- Before you start writing, use the format on this page to help you to plan and write notes.
- Allow time to read your work and check your use of language before you finish.

The argument	
Arguments for paying to watch football on television	Arguments against paying to watch football on television
Summary	

Hint: Whatever your opinion, you need to be aware of the arguments against it so that you can prepare for them.

80

The REAL THING...

> **Minor task**
>
>
> - You should spend about 25 minutes on this.
> - There are 20 marks available.
>
> **Make up a football chant to support a team of your choice.**

Think about these points:
- words of encouragement for your team
- words to tell opposing teams that your team cannot be beaten, that it will win the FA Cup, the Premiership, or another competition
- referring to your team's nickname and the team colours
- making up a chorus
- the tune: the chant could be sung to a well-known tune. If so, say which one.

Planning

- Before you start writing, use the format on this page to help you to plan and write notes. You do not need to use all the suggested ideas.
- Allow time to read your work and check your use of language and punctuation before you finish.

Chorus
Verse 1
Verse 2
Verse 3

Test Paper 6: Reading

News

Some BASICS...

This section of the paper is a test of reading and interpretation, although *how* you communicate information is important. The theme linking these three reading texts is 'News'.

- You have 1 hour and 15 minutes to answer the questions on the three passages.
- You are given 15 minutes' reading time before this.

Reading test 1
Reading and interpreting a passage from *The Seeing Stone* by Kevin Crossley-Holland

This novel is set during the reign of King Richard I ('Cœur-de-Lion', 'Lionheart', who lived from 1157–1199). It mentions real people and places and some real events, but it is fictional, since the details and some of the characters have been invented by the author. The narrator is Arthur de Caldicot, a young boy from a noble family who live in the Welsh Marches (the border area between England and Wales).

We heard bad news today.

Just before dinner one of Lord Stephen's riders galloped in. My father gave him leave to speak, and he told us King Richard has been badly wounded. A French arrow went in through his left shoulder at the base of his neck, and came out through his back.

Then we all started asking questions at the same time, and the messenger did his best to answer them.

'In the southwest of France, ma'am … a castle on a hilltop … Chalus … I don't know, sir … one of Count Aimar's …'

'Will he live?' asked Serle.

'Lord God gives life and Lord God takes it away,' my father observed.

'Lord Stephen says you will know what to do,' said the rider.

'Indeed we do,' said my father. 'We'll light candles. We'll get down on our knee-bones. Every man-jack living in this manor.'

My grandmother Nain slowly sucked in her breath.

'What is it, Nain?' asked my father rather wearily.

'What is it with your kings?' my grandmother asked in her sing-song Welsh voice. 'Harold first. An arrow through his right eye. Then Rufus, nailed to his own saddle. And now, Cœur-de-Lion.'

'If King Richard dies, it will be three times the worse for us,' said my father. 'A new king means a new tax. Remember what we had to pay so Cœur-de-Lion could fight Saladin for the kingdom of Jerusalem. The Saladin tithe!'

'You Englishman!' cried my mother, flaring up like a candle that hasn't been properly trimmed. 'Your king is dying and all you do is talk about money.'

'I didn't know the Welsh cared much for King Richard,' said my father, smiling.

My mother's eyes filled with tears. 'He brought home a piece of the Holy Cross, didn't he?'

'Sir William taught me a poem about that,' said Serle:

> 'Hot wind! Flags and banners streaming!
> Helmets shining, broadswords gleaming!
> Who can stop him, Coeur de Lion?
>   Cry Cœur-de-Lion! Jerusalem!
>
> But thirty thousand Saracen troops,
> Some alone, some in large groups,
> Hoot and jeer him, Coeur de Lion.
>   Cry Cœur-de-Lion! Jerusalem !'

'You see, John?' cried my mother. 'He's no king of mine, but he roared and rattled the gates of the Saracens.'

'Which is more than his younger brother will ever do,' said my father. 'Prince John's not half the man his elder brother was.'

'That often happens,' said my mother.

I could feel Serle was staring at me, but I didn't look back at him.

'Far better King Richard's nephew became king,' my father said. 'Prince Arthur.'

'Arthur!' I exclaimed.

Test Paper 6: Reading

'But he's only a boy,' my father continued. 'I fear for England if John is crowned king. And especially, I fear for us here in the March. The Welsh are like dogs. They can always smell a weakness.'

'Did you hear that, Nain?' my mother asked.

'Speak up!' said Nain.

'John says there'll be trouble.'

'Double?'

'No, mother. Trouble! Welsh trouble.'

'It's the English who cause trouble,' Nain said sharply. 'Years and years of it. Generations!'

This afternoon, the sky bellowed. The day darkened and quivered but the rain never came. It would have been better if it had.

Then Sir William's freeman, Thomas, rode in, and he brought the same news. The same but different. He told us King Richard had ridden up to the hilltop castle at Chalus with a dozen men, right up to the portcullis, and that one of the king's own crossbowmen, supporting him from behind, fired short. 'His bolt fell short of the battlements,' said Thomas, 'and it pierced the top of the king's back. It came out through his neck … No! Not a French arrow. It was Norman or English. It was loyal fire!'

Questions 1–8 are about *The Seeing Stone*

1 Find and copy three details from the passage which tell you that this book has a historical setting.

(1 mark)

Focus: Describe, select and retrieve information and events or ideas from the text. Use quotation and reference to the text.

The question asks you to 'find and copy', so you should quote the actual words. Look for clues such as people's names, weapons and the ways in which news was communicated. Note that you are asked for three clues only.

2 Why has the writer used ellipses in the following sentence?

(2 marks)

'In the southwest of France, ma'am … a castle on a hilltop … Chalus …. I don't know, sir … one of Count Aimar's …'

Focus: Comment on the writer's use of language, grammatical and literary features at word and sentence level.

84

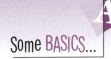

Some BASICS...

An ellipsis (plural: *ellipses*) is a set of three dots used as a punctuation mark. This question tests your knowledge of the ways in which punctuation is used to convey meaning. Comment on the way it helps you to read the words as they would have been spoken.

---

3   What does the messenger tell you in the broken sentence in question 2? Write three sentences to express it more clearly. **(2 marks)**

Focus: Deduce, infer and interpret information and events or ideas from the text.

First read the three paragraphs before the messenger speaks and work out what the people must have asked him. You can then work out what his answers mean.

---

4   Copy and complete the chart below to summarise what the passage tells you about the characters who appear in the passage. **(2 marks)**

Name, if known	Description (for example, approximate age) and other information	Relationship to the narrator, if known

Focus: Describe, select and retrieve information and events or ideas from the text. Use quotation and reference to the text.

The information you need can be found throughout the passage. In the exam you can underline the relevant sections. Use your own words when completing the chart.

Hint: For some characters you might only be given a description or their relationship to the narrator.

---

5   Which other kings had been injured by arrows before King Richard? **(1 mark)**

Focus: Describe, select and retrieve information and events or ideas from the text. Use quotation and reference to the text.

85

Test Paper 6: Reading

The narrator's grandmother gives the answer to this question. You are given only the nicknames of the kings. You do not need to work out their real names.

---

6 Explain in your own words what the narrator's father means when he says: 'We'll light candles. We'll get down on our knee-bones. Every man-jack living in this manor'. Why did he want to do this? **(2 marks)**

Focus: Deduce, infer and interpret information and events or ideas from the text.

This is testing if you understand difficult words or figures of speech and can write sentences to explain them. You can use a dictionary now, but not in an exam. A dictionary of idioms or figures of speech will help you.

---

7 Comment on the similarities and differences between the first and the second messages which are brought to the family, and the ways in which they are presented. **(2 marks)**

Focus: Deduce, infer and interpret information and events or ideas from the text.

Your answer to question 2 will help. Also look at the long paragraph which begins 'Then Sir William's freeman ….'. You should write what you notice about the messages and support it by reference to the text.

---

8 How well does the writer communicate the contrasting reactions of the characters to the death of the king?
You should write about:
- how the writer sets the tone of the passage (and describe the tone)
- the way in which information is given about characters and events (for example, through narrative and dialogue)
- the use of humour (look for the humour and describe its effect in a passage which is about the announcement of a tragic incident). **(4 marks)**

Focus: Identify and comment on the writer's purposes and viewpoints, and the effect of the text on the reader.

Bad news is brought to the characters in the passage, and the writer concentrates on their reaction to the news and how it affects them. How do the reactions of the characters match the gravity of the news? How does the writer use humour?

86

Test Paper 6: Reading

Extending Your SKILLS...

Reading test 2

Reading and interpreting a poem by Tom Leonard

This is not the Six O'Clock News, *of course – it is a poem! It is written in the way in which it is meant to be spoken.*

Unrelated Incidents 3

this is thi
six a clock
news thi
man said n
thi reason
a talk wia
BBC accent
iz coz yi
widny wahnt
mi ti talk
aboot thi
trooth wia
voice lik
wanna yoo
scruff. if
a toktaboot
thi trooth
lik wana yoo
scruff yi
widny thingk
it wuz troo.
jist wanna yoo
scruff tokn.
thirza right
way ti spell
ana right way
ti tok it. this
is me tokn yir
right way a
spellin. this
is ma trooth.
yooz doant no
thi trooth
yirsellz cawz
yi canny talk
right. this is
the six a clock
nyooz. belt up.

87

Test Paper 6: Reading

Questions 9–16 are about *Unrelated Incidents 3*

---

9   The poem is written in the way in which it should be spoken. Rewrite in standard English the part which ends at the first full stop.   **(2 marks)**

Focus: Comment on the structure and organisation of texts, grammatical and presentational features at text level.

Notice that although the part of the poem which you are asked to rewrite ends with a full stop it is, in fact, more than one sentence. This question tests your knowledge of grammar punctuation. You should punctuate it carefully.

Hint: Use full stops, commas, quotation marks and capital letters. Set the text out as it would appear in standard English. Change spellings where necessary.

---

10   Comment on the difference you made to the part of the poem which you rewrote in standard English. Explain why the poet wrote it as he did.   **(2 marks)**

Focus: Comment on the structure and organisation of texts, grammatical and presentational features at text level.

Your answer to question 1 will help. It also helps if you read both versions of the beginning of the poem aloud. You cannot do this in an exam, but you can imagine yourself reading it aloud and try to 'hear the words in your head'.

---

11   What does the poet mean by a 'BBC accent'?   **(1 mark)**

Focus: Deduce, infer and interpret information and events or ideas from the text.

This question tests your vocabulary and understanding of figures of speech. You can guess the meaning of this expression and then check it by looking at its context.

Extending Your SKILLS...

12 According to the poem, why do newsreaders have to read the news in
a 'BBC accent'? **(2 marks)**

Focus: Comment on the writer's use of language, grammatical and literary features at word and
sentence level.

Read the first fifteen lines of the poem carefully. It tells you the answer to this
question. You should write the answer in your own words, but you can support
it by quoting from the poem.

Hint: Your answer to question 9 will help.

13 According to the poem, why do the people to whom the newsreader is
speaking not know the truth? **(2 marks)**

Focus: Identify and comment on the writer's purposes and viewpoints, and the effect of the text
on the reader.

Read lines 32–36 carefully. They tell you the answer to this question. You
should write the answer in your own words, but you can support it by quoting
from the poem.

14 Select and copy a sentence, clause or phrase which suggests that the
newsreader does not respect the listeners, and explain how it does so.
(2 marks)

Focus: Deduce, infer and interpret information and events or ideas from the text.

You are asked to select and copy; this means that you should quote from the
text, but in your explanation you should write using your own words in clearly
expressed sentences.

15 What is the message of the poem? **(3 marks)**

Focus: Deduce, infer and interpret information and events or ideas from the text.

89

Test Paper 6: Reading

Write the message of the poem in your own words. This question tests your ability to express your ideas in clearly-written sentences. You should support your ideas by referring to the words of the poem.

Hint: Think about what the poem is saying about people in positions of authority and ordinary people, and about social class.

16 How successful is the poem in expressing views about social class, as shown by the way in which people speak?
You should write about:
- the views expressed in the poem
- how these views are expressed
- the effects of the layout, language and punctuation used. **(4 marks)**

Focus: Identify and comment on the writer's purposes and viewpoints, and the effect of the text on the reader.

Your answers to the other questions, especially question 15, will help. Notice what the newsreader actually says to the listeners. What does this suggest about his view of their intelligence?

| Test Paper 6: Reading

Reading test 3
Reading and interpreting a non-fiction passage

This article appeared in The Guardian *newspaper on 29 October 2002.*

Chicken fat to power lorries
By Martin Wainwright

The supermarket firm unwittingly at the centre of a cooking-oil car fuel scam has decided to try running its own fleet of lorries on waste from kitchen frying pans.

Starting in January, Asda trucks of up to 40 tonnes will carry startling slogans saying 'This vehicle is powered by chicken fat' – the biggest boost yet for the legal use of recycled cooking oil on Britain's roads.

Lorries making deliveries on Tyneside and in Yorkshire will be the first to try the fuel, which is currently available on three forecourts in Yorkshire. A further eight garages in the region are to take supplies from the growing number of biodiesel refiners, who were given a 20p-a-litre green tax concession by the Chancellor, Gordon Brown, in July.

Asda produces more than 50m litres of used cooking oil and 138,000 litres of waste frying fat every year from its canteens, restaurants and rotisseries. The gunge was a disposal headache rather than a potential money-earner until an unexpected phone call last spring.

Test Paper 6: Reading

"We were approached by a biodiesel firm, which cleans up waste cooking oil, adds a bit of methanol and sells it as a much cheaper alternative to diesel," said Rachel Fellows of Asda yesterday. "We were only too happy to do business with them.

"But then we thought: hang on, isn't there something we can do here for ourselves?"

Company trials of 'chip pan fuel' for Asda's cars and lorries were then intensified after the firm's innocent involvement last month in a moonshine operation at Llanelli in South Wales. A special 'frying squad' set up by Dyfed Powys police discovered that hundreds of drivers were running their cars on Asda's 'extra-value' cooking oil mixed with methanol at home, in a moonshine operation which dodged tax.

The 32p-a-litre fuel supply – compared with 73p at forecourt diesel pumps – was cut off when Asda discovered its Llanelli branch was selling vastly more oil than anywhere else in the country. Rationing was imposed and the police frying squad – whose tactics included sniffing out the chip-shop smell of bootleg cars – moved in.

The planned Asda fleet fuel, like all commercial biodiesel, is completely legal but will still undercut conventional diesel prices by at least 10p a litre. Converting an in-house product like the waste oil will add to savings for the firm.

"Oil's a finite resource and we are fully aware of the fact that we shouldn't be wasting it," Ms Fellows said. "This is real eco-innovation – trials already show that chip pan fuel emissions are up to 40% lower than diesel."

Questions 17–23 are about *Chicken fat to power lorries*

17 Find and copy three pieces of information which suggest why chicken fat is a better fuel than conventional diesel oil.　　　　　　　　　　**(2 marks)**

Focus: Describe, select and retrieve information and events or ideas from the text. Use quotation and reference to the text.

There are several reasons suggested in the passage as to why chicken fat is a better fuel than diesel. You should quote only three of them. You are asked to 'find and copy', so you need to quote the actual words. Don't forget quotation marks.

92

Over to YOU...

18 What do you think 'biodiesel' means? **(1 mark)**

Focus: Deduce, infer and interpret information and events or ideas from the text.

You can use a dictionary in class (but not in an exam) to look up the meaning of this word (or of its prefix and root word). It is a new word and therefore might not be in your dictionary, but you can work out its meaning from the root word and the prefix and from the context in which it is used.

19 Find and copy two phrases in paragraph 4 which have opposite meanings. Explain their meanings. **(2 marks)**

Focus: Describe, select and retrieve information and events or ideas from the text. Use quotation and reference to the text.

Consider the context in which the phrases are used and in what ways their meanings are opposites in this context. Think about what they meant to Asda.

20 Explain the play on words in 'frying squad'. Describe the picture it creates in your mind. **(2 marks)**

Focus: Comment on the writer's use of language, grammatical and literary features at word and sentence level.

A play on words links two ideas; you should think about what two things are being linked and how appropriate the link is. You should comment on what makes the word-play humorous.

When you are asked to describe the picture created in your mind there is no 'right answer' as long as you use the information from the poem, so don't be afraid to explain how you have reacted to the image in the poem.

Hint: Remember: a play on words can be a pun or the use of similar-sounding words in which their meanings are relevant to the context.

Test Paper 6: Reading

21 Find and copy as many words or phrases as you can which are used as nouns for the new fuel.

(2 marks)

Focus: Describe, select and retrieve information and events or ideas from the text. Use quotation and reference to the text

You should skim-read the passage to find words and phrases used to refer to the new fuel. This question tests your ability to find information in the text. It also tests your understanding of the terms 'words', 'phrases' and 'nouns'. You are asked to 'find and copy', so you should quote from the passage (using quotation marks).

Hint: Skim-read the entire passage.

22 Explain why the reporter uses so many different words and phrases for the same fuel.

(2 marks)

Focus: Deduce, infer and interpret information and events or ideas from the text.

Remember that the fuel is a new one and many of the words for similar fuels are so new that they might not be in dictionaries. What help might the reporter be trying to give to the readers?

23 How successful has the writer been in attracting the attention of readers and keeping their attention throughout the report?
You could write about:
- how interesting and amusing the headline is
- how well the introduction attracts attention and sets the scene for the report
- the writer's explanation of the new fuel to non-specialist readers (how clear is it and how interesting?)
- the use of humour
- the pace of the report.

(5 marks)

Focus: Identify and comment on the writer's purposes and viewpoints, and the effect of the text on the reader.

How did you respond to the report? Did you enjoy it? If so, what did you enjoy about it? Trust your own responses and then explain them, using references to the report to support your answers.

You have already commented on many of the points in your answers to the previous questions.

| Test Paper 6: Writing

The REAL THING...

Writing test

These two writing assignments are linked to the theme of 'News'.

Major task

- You should spend about 40 minutes on this.
- There are 30 marks available.

Write a fictional recount of the response of a family or another group of people in modern times to a piece of news.

Think about these points:
- basing your fictional recount on a real event
- modelling your writing on the passage
- using dialogue to present the news and the characters' reactions to it (and their responses to one another's comments)
- using dialogue to reveal what interests the characters.

Planning

- Before you start writing, use the format on this page to help you to plan and write notes.
- Allow time to read your work and check your use of language before you finish.

Title		
The news		
Characters Names, relationships to one another, other information about them		**Setting** Time Place
Characters' reactions to the news		
Character		**Reaction**
Ending		

95

Test Paper 6: Writing

Minor task

- You should spend about 25 minutes on this.
- There are 20 marks available.

Write a rap about a news item you have heard. Tell the news.

Think about these points:
- keeping the rap short
- writing standard English (not non-standard English, for example, like that of the poem 'Unrelated Incidents 3'), although you could model the rhythm of your rap on the poem
- a rap does not need to rhyme, although it can if you want it to.

Planning

- Before you start writing, use the format on this page to help you to plan the scene.
- Allow time to read your work and check your use of language and punctuation before you finish.

The news
The story in note form

Hint: Try more than one idea for each part of the rap.

Opening line

Middle of the rap

Ending

96